SPEAKERS OF LIFE

How to live an everyday prophetic lifestyle

Mark Birch-Machin PhD, BSc

RIVER
PUBLISHING

River Publishing & Media Ltd
info@river-publishing.co.uk

ISBN 978-1-908393-43-2
Cover design by www.SpiffingCovers.com

Contents

Dedication

In memory of Dorothy Vickers, a powerful,
inspirational, loving and generous woman of God,
whose life and ministry clearly reflected
that she had "been with Jesus".

Part of Dorothy's rich voyage was to inspire,
unlock and mentor people. I was privileged to be
one of those who Dorothy encouraged to fly higher in the
prophetic and whose advice, "to keep my heart soft", has been
the single, most valuable key to unlocking the prophetic gift.
Thank you for handing over this baton.

What Others Are Saying About This Book...

"I have always known Mark to be wildly enthusiastic, yet sensitive, brilliant, yet simple, mature, yet totally child-like, extremely wise, yet totally teachable! You will find such combinations of qualities flowing forth from this book.

Mark takes what others often make complicated and super-spiritualized and shows us the reality, the possibility and the adventure of carrying the Holy Spirit's life-giving words into the market place, mostly to those outside the confines of religious boxes. You will be encouraged to become a "speaker of life" in your own Christian walk."

Mary Audrey Raycroft
Founder of Releasers of Life Equipping Ministries
Teaching Pastor, Catch the Fire, Toronto, Canada

"Ten years ago, Mark helped me set up St Luke's Newcastle, and from that moment to this I have remained amazed at his sensitivity to the Spirit's voice. He has an extraordinary gift in teaching the prophetic to all who would learn. Mark, with his lovely, gentle but sharp personality endears himself to all with ears to hear and hearts to receive. I'm sure, now, those with eyes to read and minds to be renewed will love the material in this book and the manner in which he spreads out the riches of the prophetic walk. As his pastor, and as leader of the Charismatic and Pentecostal church leaders in Newcastle, I can confirm that he truly walks the walk as he talks the talk!"

Rev Dr Robert Ward,
Vicar of St Luke's, Newcastle Upon Tyne

"Mark's book takes us on an inspirational journey into the prophetic. He demystifies prophecy and explains how it can operate naturally in our day-to-day lives. Speakers of Life is informative, immensely practical and peppered with challenging stories which leave the reader thinking, 'I can do that!'."

Diana Chapman,
River Church Thames Valley, Author *Britain's Spiritual Inheritance*

"Best friends love sharing their secrets, and hearing God share His secrets with us is probably the greatest privilege we can ever experience. Mark's quality of friendship is outstanding and makes this remarkable book on learning, not only how to hear God's voice in all arenas of life, but competently handling what God shares, just so fantastic. This book gives you the tools to speak life to your world."

Duncan Smith,
Co-founder Catch The Fire World, Senior Leader CTF Raleigh, USA

Acknowledgements

Speakers of Life is all about Jesus. We are united and serve under the wonderful, glorious, loving name of Jesus. Therefore, SOL is an ongoing story of all our lives, affected by the living flame of love and He deserves all the glory.

My journey continues to be one of saying "thanks" and "more Lord" for all the help I have received The list of people is, of course, extensive, ranging from those who have walked with me for many years to those brief God-encounters with those from whom I have received a wonderful life-changing word. It's difficult to list everyone, but here is the tip of the "thank you iceberg".

First and foremost I am privileged to be part of the most wonderful and totally fun family: Juliet, my wife of 30 years marriage (August 2014) who first introduced me to Jesus; then my two sons, Joel and Sam, who ensure that I do not take myself too seriously. Without their incredible help and encouragement, the first few years of Friday night SOL meetings in our house, where we might have up to 65 people turning up hungry for God (and food!), would have been very different. And thank you, of course, to my parents, Roy and Irene for their continual encouragement.

Thanks to the people who have journeyed with me in my Christian walk to date, in particular John Arnott, Duncan Smith, Ken and Lois Gott, Robert and Alice Ward, Mary Audrey Raycroft, Laurel Hobbs, Alan and Ann Finlay, Andrew and Alena Warburton, Sandy Dirks, Randy Vickers, Sola and Liz Idowu, Joy Ogwu, David and Karen Vickers, Liz Palmer, Anna Spencer, Tom and Cindy Deboer, Nathan "Shakka" Norris, and Minty.

Thank you to my amazing SOL Council of Reference made up of church leaders, past and present, namely Paul Fenwick (and "The Family"), Alan Dickinson, David Bedford, Rob Hawkins and David Vickers. Thank you to the wider support family of church leaders from Together in Christ (Tyneside) and particularly to those who have accommodated SOL gatherings in their church buildings to welcome the prophetic in the region (thanks particularly to Clive Devonish, Mark Elder and Simon Lawton).

Thank you to the pioneering leaders of the four SOLs we have planted from the original SOL in Newcastle, Tyneside, which now incorporate around 100 churches. Thanks to Richard and Denise Morrison for leading the three SOLs in Northern Ireland (Newcastle, Kilkeel and Portadown) and to Eunice Brennan and Fred Rudkin for leading the SOL in Barnard Castle (County Durham). There are more SOLs in the pipeline! In addition, it's wonderful to see that people in other churches, where we have had input over the years, have independently begun to mimic and apply the vision and principles of SOL life in their own context and community.

Thanks to Karen who, out of thousands of people, just "happened" to bump into Di Chapman, who I then subsequently met and who introduced me to her publisher, the lovely Tim of River Publishing; this book was always part of God's plan.

Thank you to my spiritual family in Bethel Church, Redding, USA; the Barnsleys, Metcalfes and Claire McCourt, you are all an inspiration. Thanks particularly to Nic Barnsley, Jenny "from Jersey" Portijo, Sandy Dirks, the prophets from Glasgow prophetic centre, Northumbrian Centre of Prayer for Christian Healing who prophetically encouraged me to write this book (and more).

Thanks to Ali Durrant for the excellent documentation of the events and stories of the monthly SOL gatherings over the years, and to Lisa "Amigo" Jacobs for typing the testimonies for the book, and to the same Lisa and Ali with Karen Vickers, Marcus Durrant, Sue Hook, my wife Juliet, Fred Rudkin and Lynne Gowland for proof reading the chapters.

Finally, thanks to all the SOL family to whom this book belongs, and for making the leading of SOL a profound honour, privilege and joy.

Opening Prayer

We welcome you Father, Abba, Daddy God.

We welcome you Lord Jesus.

We welcome you Holy Spirit.

Angels of God, we thank and praise God that

he has sent you to help us; you are also welcome

Love of God come!

Kingdom of Heaven come, on earth, right now!

Preface

All stories in this book are provided by the author or members of Speakers of Life and have been written in the first person narrative to ensure anonymity and that all the credit and glory goes to Jesus. This is one of the hallmarks of Speakers of Life, whose members come from many Christian denominations and streams. As the leader, I encourage members to record and send the details of their God-encounters to me. Then I and others (e.g. my council of reference) verify the stories and apply the "anonymous brush" to the account, circulating it on Facebook and via our mailing list for encouragement and faith building. Apart from me and the leadership team, no one knows the identity of the people in the stories and Jesus gets all the credit. It is, after all, all about him! Our desire is for people to know, belong to and trust Jesus – the focus being on him and not us.

As a scientist, I am trained in evidence-based claims. These stories have therefore been verified to the best of our abilities by several independent witnesses and the recipient. To facilitate this process we have been diligent, over the last 4-5 years, in recording all that happens during our Friday night meetings and our prophecy-on-the-streets adventures. We do this to be faithful to the "recording" principle laid down in Habakkuk 2:2 and to steward the precious testimonies God gives us, so that they can be fruitful at the appointed time (Habakkuk 2:3). In addition, Scripture teaches us that if we are faithful with the small things, God will give us more and more to steward (Matthew 25:21-23) and bless us with a spiritual "upgrade" (Deuteronomy 28:1-14).

The aim of this book

This book is about activating and training the prophetic in each one of us, so that we can take prophecy beyond the walls of the church, out onto the streets, to bless people and to speak the life of Jesus to our communities and our land.

We want to see churches, full of vibrant sons and daughters of the living God, emptied onto the streets. As the current Pope Francis wrote during his previous position as Archbishop of Buenos Aires:

"We need to avoid the spiritual sickness of a church that is wrapped up in its own world. When a church becomes like this, it grows sick. It is true that going out onto the streets implies the risk of accidents happening, as they would to any ordinary man or woman. But if the church stays wrapped up in itself, it will age. And if I had to choose between a wounded church that goes out onto the streets and a sick withdrawn church, I would definitely choose the first one."

1

The Birth And Vision Of Speakers Of Life (SOL)

Purpose and aims

Originally founded in our home in Newcastle upon Tyne, UK, in November 2009, Speakers of Life (or SOL from here onwards) is a prophetic group of Christians from approximately 100 churches who are seeking to sharpen their prophetic gifting to serve and equip the Church, and to bless their communities by sharing God's love through prophecy on the streets.

As you will see throughout this book, SOL is so much more than a school of prophets. Many Christians are already hearing God's voice, but often don't recognise it. SOL therefore encourages believers to practice hearing God's voice and apply this to their lives. More importantly, we encourage them to practice acting on God's voice outside as well as inside the Church, with the purpose of being a blessing to those who may not know the love of God. The vision of SOL is twofold:

1. To serve others by sharpening their prophetic edge or gifting (as iron sharpens iron, Proverbs 27:17) for the benefit of their local churches, and so that they in turn may encourage, train and equip others.

2. To serve as a prophetic voice, speaking the life of Jesus so as to bless and prosper the Church, our cities, our regions, our nation and other nations.

At its heart, SOL is all about unity; to bring together Christians from many streams to be a service to both church and community. As evangelist J. John often says, "None of us have got it all together, but together we have all got it."

There are currently five official SOL centres: two in England (one in Newcastle upon Tyne, led by myself, and another in Barnard Castle led by Fred Rudkin and Eunice Brennan) and three in Northern Ireland (in Newcastle, Portadown and Kilkeel, led by Richard and Denise Morrison). There are a number of others in the pipeline linked to SOL "family members" in various parts of the USA and on other continents, and other churches in the UK who have been encouraged and inspired by our visits have begun their own prophetic "speaking life" activities.

A brief history

The first meeting of SOL happened in our converted garage with seven people representing three different churches on November 13, 2009. It was the result of the direct encouragement and prophetic input of a number of international church leaders, but particularly John Arnott (who with his wife, Carol, are the founding pastors and presidents of Catch the Fire) and also Duncan Smith (who with his wife, Kate, are vice-presidents of Catch the Fire and directors of CTF USA).

About twelve months before the start of SOL, God had been increasingly speaking to me about creating a space and place for people to come for prophetic training in unity – somewhere that would equip them to minister God's love to bless others both inside and outside of the Church. I had sat on this for a while and, as with all steps of faith, sometimes one needs a polite "kick up the pants" to motivate us to action.

This "moment of encouragement" came in the form of the lovely John Arnott. Over a spontaneous lunch in the CTF church in Toronto, John more or less paraphrased what God had been prompting me to do over the previous twelve months and firmly encouraged me to do it as the next step in my prophetic journey. I was well known by John and others in CTF for my prophetic gifting. I also had an established prophetic track record amongst churches in the north east of England. For a while I had been leading prophetic training days, retreats, preaching at other churches, and had occupied prophetic leadership roles in churches led by Ken and Lois Gott and my current church (St Luke's, Newcastle, led by Robert Ward).

To date, I'd had the privilege of being mentored in the prophetic by a number of people – but notably Lois Gott and the late Dorothy Vickers (co-founder with her husband, Revd. Randolph Vickers, of the Northumbrian Centre of Prayer For Christian Healing and the lady to whom this book is dedicated). Both encouraged me to spread and use my prophetic wings. Now, through John, God was encouraging me to take the next step.

The next step

I knew I had to be obedient to what God was prompting me to do. As Jean Darnell prophesied, alluding to Paul's words in Acts 26:19, "Obedience releases the vision" (see Ch4). So I asked God, "How do I start?" and "Who do I invite?"

The answer came to find and invite like-minded people who shared the same spiritual DNA – those in which one could discern in the Spirit, the "sound of rushing waters (Revelation 1:15, 14:2;

Ezekiel 43:2). In Hebrew, the word for prophet is *nabi*, the root of which means "to bubble forth, as from a fountain" (we'll discuss this more in Ch3). I wanted to gather together those in whom the word of God was bubbling up and the first meeting was all about welcoming, in unity, the presence of God and speaking out the life-giving word of God.

The day after our first meeting, the name "Speakers of Life" came to me during my morning jog. I was reflecting on the previous night and realised that was what we had been doing all evening. SOL, it's abbreviated form, also means "sun" in Spanish and I couldn't help but see the parallels between the natural sun that gives life and the Son of God, Jesus, who gives us eternal life (John 3:16). The name also resonated with the network called "Releasers of Life" led by my good friend, Mary Audrey Raycroft in CTF Toronto.

I knew immediately after that first night that the Lord would grow SOL quickly and so by the time of the second meeting a month later, I already had a council of reference in place. When any new ministry emerges, it is so important that proper accountability is put in place to keep everything on track. The original council of reference consisted of the local charismatic Anglican vicar, David Bedford of All Saints Gosforth, in whose parish our house was located (geographic accountability); a charismatic Methodist minister, Rob Hawkins of Jesmond Methodist Church; and the last member to join was the pastor of the Bay Church, Whitley Bay, Alan Dickinson. Alan remains on the current council with Paul Fenwick, Pastor of Byker City Fellowship International, and David Vickers, Leader of the Northumbrian Centre of Prayer For Christian Healing.

The fruit of the first meetings

As we focussed on the two aims of SOL (to sharpen each other's prophetic gifting and to be a voice to bless the city) one of our members was given a revelation of a detailed spiritual map of Newcastle City. We worked through this, diligently confirming and recording the details (per Habakkuk 2:2-3) and handed it to our council of reference to steward. The "map" was then shared via the council to the Together in Christ Tyneside (TiC) network, since our council of reference members were, and currently are, part of this network.

TiC consists of 35-40 charismatic church leaders in the city (coordinated by Rev Dr Robert Ward) working together in Newcastle under the banner of "one church, many denominations". In due course they gave us some feedback and reported that members of TiC who had been pastors in the city for years had been amazed at how accurate was the spiritual map. This was further confirmed by the leader of the local branch of Street Pastors who were out on the streets all the time. All that TiC knew is that the revelation came from SOL, via our council, and this anonymity meant that all the credit went to Jesus and the city was blessed. I'll say it again: it's all about him! That's why, during the first 4-5 years of SOL's establishment and growth there have never been any names mentioned on our website or Facebook page, other than the name of Jesus!

Further growth

As a result of this initial contact I was asked to represent SOL at the TiC city pastor network. This brought the benefit of wider accountability, as SOL became an associated ministry of TiC, alongside Healing on the Streets and Street Pastors. It also meant that, as well as our council of reference, we could now build relationships with 35-40 other church leaders. It followed that many of SOL's original members were drawn from these churches, as well as associated network churches, since we were considered a "secure place" for church leaders to encourage their congregation to go to be activated, trained and stretched in the prophetic. Since SOL is not a church but a "neutral" organisation serving all the churches, the leaders could be assured of getting their congregation back!

During the first two-and-a-half years the neutral venue for our monthly Friday evening SOL meetings continued to be our home. In addition to the members of the regional TiC churches, we routinely had people making the 100-120 mile round trip from the west coast of England and the Scottish borders. When you are hungry, you are prepared to be inconvenienced in order to be fed and receive! We love to bless church leaders, so it was wonderful to have regular opportunities to bless them and deliver prophetic encouragement. As many of the leaders said: "Where else can I go to be blessed and to receive personal prophecy from so many people that do not know my situation?" Many of the leaders remarked upon the amazing accuracy of the words that were given. It was unusual for them to be able to come to a safe place, where they could simply be a child of the living God (and not "on duty" as a leader) and they were overwhelmed by the half-dozen pages of prophetic words of love which they would walk away with, back to their own church and congregation.

More people began to attend the Friday night meetings and our family (my wife, Juliet, and our sons Joel and Sam) had to create more space in every downstairs room to accommodate sixty-five people engaging with God in the kitchen, the hallway (some didn't make it into the rest of the house as they ended up on the floor under the presence of God in the hallway) and any other space they could find. We didn't know who was going to walk through the door and we provided buffet food for whoever came to help people to mix and be comfortable with each other. People would begin to arrive from 7.30pm and we would start the gathering at around 8.15pm, but really God was already working while people were eating and talking.

People were healed and delivered of all manner of things during these times. Others just couldn't stand as the presence of God was so heavy. The worship was, and has always been, spontaneous and the teams have always comprised worshippers from different churches. There has often been a seamless transition as different people have taken over playing various instruments – sometimes even half way through a song as, for example, our keyboard player or guitarist will slowly slide to the ground under the power of the Holy Spirit.

Although we officially finished at 10pm, many would continue to encounter God in our house until the early hours of the morning and the presence of God was very tangible in the house for many days afterwards. The prophetic training that took place during these evenings and the stories of what happened when we took it onto the streets is detailed in the rest of the book.

Eventually, we concluded that we didn't want the size of our house to limit the growth of SOL and, with amazing timing, a number of leaders offered their churches for our monthly Friday night meetings. We took up every offer, so that we could "tabernacle", moving from church to church each month. It meant that we could cover the geography not only of the city, but also the areas east to the coast, and west to the more rural river Tyne valley. This provided numerous opportunities to bless many churches, the land, and to open up historic spiritual wells – particularly as our region in the north east of England was one of the main gateways to Christianity in Britain in the 7th Century via St Aidan, Cuthbert and the Celtic monks. For those who are not familiar with its history, there is a rich heritage to explore in this "cradle of Christianity" that is perhaps best left for a follow up book. Meanwhile, you can read the excellent books Britain's Spiritual Inheritance by Diana Chapman (River Publishing) and Fire of the North by David Adam (SPCK).

As we continued to grow, we gave our blessing to a wonderful South African family, the Morrisons, to plant a SOL in Northern Ireland (in a town also called Newcastle). Moving in the favour of God, Richard and Denise Morrison quickly established a gathering place with the core values of SOL and people from different Protestant and Catholic churches came. Within twelve months they planted another SOL in Portadown, some 35 miles away, and have now established a third in Kilkeel. God is in the business of equipping and raising people up to be leaders, regardless of whether or not they have done anything like that in the past. Similarly, Fred Rudkin and Eunice Brennan, "got out of the boat" in faith to plant Barnard Castle SOL in another county 50 miles away from us. This is going extremely well as Christians from different churches ride the wave of unity and command a blessing on their community.

All these SOL plants have a regular monthly meeting where people come to be encouraged and trained in the prophetic, as well as express worship and prophetic art, and then apply this to bless people on the streets. The style of the evenings may differ from plant to plant, but the core aims and mission remain the same – speaking words which release life and quickly shape a godly lifestyle. As the Scriptures say:

"The words I have spoken to you – they are full of the Spirit and life." (John 6:63)

"Words have power: The tongue has the power of life and death, and those who love it will eat its fruit." (Proverbs 18:21)

"If anyone says to this mountain, 'Go, throw yourself into the sea,' and does not doubt in their heart but believes that what they say will happen, it will be done for them." (Mark 11:23)

"The right word at the right time is like a custom-made piece of jewellery." (Proverbs 25:11 MSG)

"Blessed are those who listen to me, watching daily at my doors, waiting at my doorway. For those who find me find life and receive favour from the LORD." (Proverbs 8:34-35)

"If anyone speaks, he should do it as one speaking the very words of God." (1 Peter 4:11)

"The tongue that brings healing is a tree of life, but a deceitful tongue crushes the spirit." (Proverbs 15:4)

"The mouth of the righteous is a fountain of life." (Proverbs 10:11)

Wow! Let's sow and invest our time into occupying that place where we can find and hear the words of God and, indeed, the words of LIFE!

At SOL, we don't just want to encourage people to give out occasional "words" from God. We want to encourage people to live a prophetic lifestyle. Hearing from God is not to be an occasional event or a sporadic hobby we might engage in when convenient – it is part of a prophetic lifestyle that needs to be embraced and practiced. That is why this book is more than simply a manual to teach you how to use the prophetic gift – it is an invitation to join a movement of people who desire to pour out God's extravagant blessing onto the streets of their communities; to unconditionally bless, bless, bless those who may or may not know Jesus, the lover of their souls!

Riding the wave of unity is the key

A key verse in Revelation 19:10 says that, "the testimony of Jesus is the spirit of prophecy." It reminds us of the pre-eminence of Jesus is all that we do. We have no desire to establish our own authority or prominence. In this respect, unity is a principle vital to SOL's operation. We meet together under the magnificent, glorious name of Jesus and allow him to call all the shots. As Psalm 133 confirms,

"How good and pleasant it is when God's people live together in unity! It is like precious oil poured on the head, running down on the beard, running down on Aaron's beard, down on the collar of his robe. It is as if the dew of Hermon were falling on Mount Zion. For there the LORD bestows his blessing, even life forevermore."

Seeing the bigger picture

Unity is a gift that allows us to see the whole picture of what God is doing, as we see and hear the precious revelation that God has stored in other earthen vessels. Unity also allows us, due to being together with people from many different church streams, to welcome and accommodate the different ways in which God speaks to us. It allows us the opportunity to lay down our preconceived notions. The joining together of prophets leads to an amazing prophetic flow which is not usually seen in a single prophet who stays in their own cave by themselves.

At every SOL meeting we record all of the prophecies that are spoken, as we have learnt to value the treasure that God entrusts to us. This is a key tool in helping us to see the patterns in what God is saying and, if he is saying the same thing through a number of different people, to act upon them. As we do this, the prophetic community can join in unity with other intercessors (Prayer for Tyneside in our region, for example) to ask the Lord to bring about his plans and purposes for the region. Since we see in part and prophesy in part, then as we put together everyone's pieces of revelation, we can come together to see the much bigger picture (bigger than our own church) of what God is doing within a city and a region. It is just like a jigsaw puzzle, with everyone making their contribution to the prophetic destiny and history of their region. Unity is the key. No single church or network has all the pieces of the jigsaw. But every region has a prophetic destiny and we can seek God to discover it.

From the moment we had our first SOL gathering, the unity of that meeting provided us with a bigger picture – if you like, a global prophetic "neural network", of which SOL was just one part, interfacing with other prophetic networks. We captured the vision for a dynamic network where "ordinary" Spirit-filled believers (i.e. not major international speakers or leaders of large churches) would simultaneously receive revelation from God in various parts of the world and share it. Imagine a scenario in which Christians from many different streams are relaying the same revelation from God, which is noticed and acted upon, potentially so much more than a single voice coming from one individual or one Church stream. Unity means that revelation from God via the prophetic word is activated more quickly as the same message is broadcast across the globe. And, of course, the really attractive aspect of a dynamic, global neural prophetic network is that no one knows the names of the individuals who are passing on the revelation – so guess who gets the credit? You've got it, Jesus!

An easy yoke

One of the most remarkable benefits of unity is that when everyone comes together under the wonderful, mighty name of Jesus, everything works so beautifully and easily. Currently SOL encompasses around 100 churches from many diverse denominations and streams, and when we meet to serve Jesus' agenda, rather than our own, it is like riding a wave of blessing. As

Jesus himself says in Matthew 11:30, it is so easy and light. Often, as we have moved out of the church and into the community, carried on this wave of unity, people who have attended churches for years have commented how everything seems so much easier – even more fun – than they can recall it being in the past.

A safe place

A further benefit of unity is that it creates a safe place for people to be equipped. They are allowed to train and develop their gift in an environment where they have complete permission to make mistakes and also to express their gift in many diverse ways. In SOL this includes activities such as prophetic art and music, as well as spoken word ministry and prayer. Later in this book I will describe some of the methods God is using to touch the lives of others and, where appropriate, provide manual-type instructions for those who want to engage with them. These includes things such as training days for the church to nurture the prophetic in its midst, treasure hunting, business prophecy, dream interpretation, healing prayer, allowing Jesus to minister through us to people at psychic fayres, holding our own spiritual fayres for the general public, responding to invitations to pray over cities and churches, establishing connections with other prophetic networks, angelic encounters, prophetic art, worship, deliverance, governmental arenas and more!

A home for the hungry

SOL is also about finding others who are hungry (see the discussion on nurturing the prophetic in the Church in Ch8). Kevin Horn writes, "When you are learning to hear the voice of the Lord and growing in the prophetic, find a prophetic community to nurture the work of God and learn to work as a team. Otherwise, prophetic people sometimes have the tendency to be loners" (Activating Your Prophetic Gift, Open Heavens Revival Press). A special dynamic happens when hungry people gather in unity as a prophetic community to pray for their cities and church leaders. It is like Daniel asking his other prophetic friends to release revelation and understanding when pressed by King Nebuchadnezzar to interpret a dream. In the unity of seeking his voice, God hears the cry of the hungry. As Paula A. Price writes in The Prophet's Handbook (Whitaker House), when prophetic people gather to pray with their prophetic peers of like spirit, "the results are explosive. Their respective mantles collaborate, and each one's anointing and power are magnified a thousand fold."

Prophecy flourishes under godly authority

In order for the prophetic ministry to flourish, it has to function in the context of godly authority. In order to submit to and serve the body of Christ, this requires a connectedness to the five-fold ministries of Ephesians 4, as we work with and honour established pastors, apostles, evangelists and teachers in a city and region. Through SOL we want to see the prophetic restored to the main body of the Church, not existing outside of it as a peripheral, isolated ministry. One of the enemy's great tactics has been to marginalise the prophetic from the other key ministries and therefore rob the body of Christ of being fully equipped in all areas, thus limiting its maturity.

When the five-fold ministries work together, it produces a fountain of God's grace. Apostles release prophets and give them a platform from which to speak. Pastors care for the souls of the prophets so that they prophesy from healed rather than hurt hearts. Evangelists call the prophets to see the harvest fields and the beating fiery heart of God for the last, the least and the lost.

Teachers bring continual grounding in God's word to encourage the prophets to remain scriptural, and may bring connection with historical realities that confirm the words the prophets are speaking.

During a key period in October 2013, for example, SOL was involved with other ministries in our region during nine evenings of outpouring gatherings, with a desire to usher in breakthrough for our region and beyond. Whilst on the floor of our gathering place in the chandelier decorated, ornate Wallsend Hall, one SOL member heard the Holy Spirit utter the numbers 1715, 1745 and the phrases "lack of trust" and "betrayal". On delivering this to the team, the prophets and teachers discerned that this related to the exact dates of the two hotspots of the Jacobite rebellion in our region and the betrayal in 1715 of about 300 horseman and key nobles. On closer inspection it was clear that this sphere of betrayal had been evident for years and this revelation enabled us to break the demonic spirit which had been exerting its influence in this area for many centuries. Prophet and teacher working together – a potent mixture!

Speaking life changes the atmosphere

When we gather together in unity we can expect the Lord to speak to us like never before! Jeremiah 33.3 says, "Call to me and I will answer you and show you great and mighty things that you do not know." We are told to access the throne of grace boldly and confidently (Hebrews 4:16) and to expect heavenly encounters as the "door of heaven" is opened to us (Revelation 4:1). The door that John saw is still open and God calls us to "Come up here." As we do, the spiritual temperature of our environment will increase.

The breath or *ruach* of God changes the atmosphere. It has the ability to turn what appears to be dry bones into an army (Ezekiel

37). The root meaning of *ruach* is "moving air", whether in the fo of breath, a breeze or a violent wind, and represents the Spirit of God.

Paula Price comments that, "Prophets' prayer companies immediately transform their environments into a battlefield, a revelation hub, a military camp and a worship and praise centre." Importantly, she highlights the truth that, "Before tackling other issues, responsible prophets come to God to be healed, cleansed and empowered." Therefore, breakthroughs, deliverance from oppression and physical and emotional healing are amongst the normal fruit of a SOL gathering.

God's creative power is shown when his mouth speaks words: "God said, 'Let there be light'; and there was light" (Genesis 1:3). Ruach is another way of describing God's presence, because when he comes near to human beings and speaks to them, his breath and word convey his presence. If you can hear someone breathing, it means that they are close to you. Psalm 139:7 says,

"Where can I go from your Spirit, where can I flee from your Presence..."

Spirit and Presence are both derivatives of ruach. We live in exciting days where the power of speaking life is becoming a lifestyle. The Ezekiel 37 dry bones phenomenon is happening all over. Not just in a valley, but across communities and nations, and sometimes even in the most unlikely of places. As Isaiah 41:18 says,

"I will make rivers flow on barren heights, and springs within the valleys. I will turn the desert into pools of water, and the parched ground into springs."

What is the fruit of SOL?
The fruit is seen in the Church, but importantly we see it in abundance on our streets and communities. This will be discussed

il later, with numerous stories and testimonies, but
of what God is doing in people's lives:

lives. A sharper gifting and a sense and reality of
', as many SOL members have commented.

nto calling and destiny. To be what God has called
us to be and do what God called us to do. One example, which
is covered in more detail in chapters 3 and 7, is that of prophetic
confirmation (speaking into the lives of others about things that God
was already prompting in them) and experiencing accompanying
signs and wonders in our meetings. As a result of one particular
SOL meeting, a member has embarked on training to be a Catholic
priest in Rome, a journey that takes 7-10 years! This same person
recorded that he experienced "gold dust" on his hands and arms
that night, which has manifest every time he has taken the bread
and wine at his local church.

• **Salvation and discipleship.** Many people have come to Christ
and then also led others to Jesus.

• **Deliverance.** There has been freedom from demonic oppression.
People have been released to be how they were meant to be – free!
We have seen people set free from curses and other things that have
enslaved them, such as items that were given to them. The Bible
has many warnings about bringing items which represent spiritual
idols into our home (or camp in the Old Testament). Jewellery is one
example, as in the story of Achan in Joshua chapter 7. Here is one
story form a SOL member:

*"During times of soaking in God's presence I have had pictures
of rings on the fingers of people I have not seen for a while. On
contacting them, I found that their lives had taken a turn for
the worse (they themselves used the word 'cursed'). On further
questioning, it became evident that this coincided with receiving*

rings from people who turned out to be unpleasant in their lives. However, they still retained the rings, either on their person or in a jar in the house. The pictures of the rings I received during soaking exactly matched their rings. In each case, the person responded immediately by removing the ring and/or returning it, which directly correlated with an about-turn in their life for the better as they were freed from that curse."

- **Emotional and physical healing.** Because of the increased expectancy of what God can do through us achieved in SOL training, many of our members see God healing regularly on the streets, in restaurants and cafés, as part of the fruit of the prophetic lifestyle. This is further increased as we work with networks such as Healing On The Streets (see Healing On The Streets by Mark Marx, River Publshing).
- **Equipping.** Being stretched and growing in our prophetic gifting as we go beyond our comfort zone (1 Timothy 4:14-15) and not succumbing to fear (2 Timothy 1:6-7). Equipping can be achieved through individual training or through SOL training days for many churches. Overcoming fear is key, as one way the enemy seeks to keep us from the door of breakthrough is to place the demonic spirits of fear and intimidation on either side of that door.
- **Church restoration.** We see restoration in and out of the Church as churches are emptied onto the streets to spill over with the love of Jesus.
- **Community restoration.** We also see God moving to bring restoration (spiritually and financially) in workplaces, neighbourhoods, towns and cities.
- **Signs and wonders that point to Jesus.** Almost every time we meet we see gold (see When Heaven Invades Earth by Bill Johnson, Destiny Image) or oil on people's faces and hands. Not just in our

meeting places, but in the centre of McDonalds or when handing out flyers on the street. Just like the prophet Daniel, God gives us insights into people's dreams and the interpretation of those dreams, even before the people have told us about them. Coupled with healing and deliverance, this is the ultimate show and tell. For example, demonstrating God's healing power and telling the person that this is not from you, but a sign of the kingdom of the God who loves them. "Heal those there who are ill and tell them, 'The kingdom of God has come near to you.'" (Luke 10:9)

• **Changing spiritual atmosphere.** Opening up ancient wells of revival and worship without walls on the streets.

• **Entry into "closed" cultural spheres.** Open doors to speak the life of Jesus into international governmental places and underground network churches in oppressed regimes.

• **Release of provision and prosperity.** To provide strategy for businesses and release prosperity which will benefit the poor, mercy ministries etc. This can be in the form of a prophecy for a company or an individual business person in the marketplace or in the church. An example story from a SOL member may help to illustrate that a prophetic word can lead to financial release:

"I was preaching at our local church and the Lord gave me a prophetic word in the middle of the sermon, so I stopped and said that I felt the Lord was speaking to someone in the room about the fact they were in two minds about charging a particular price in a business context. I said, 'You feel obliged to charge the lower price, but you feel prompted by the Holy Spirit to charge the higher price.' The Lord then gave me the actual amounts of the two prices. A couple responded to this, saying that the numbers quoted were the exact amounts that they were deliberating over and were encouraged to go with the Holy Spirit's prompting."

There are many examples in SOL of people being prompted to give money to people who they didn't know needed the money. Moreover, the amount that was given was exactly what they needed and, in some cases, made that person debt free to the penny! One lady responded to a prophetic word about a past history of being cut in an abusive way and an invitation to let Jesus into the restoration and forgiveness aspect of this time to "cut" her free from the damage and baggage of this time in her life. This was done and the lady was changed, freed and very grateful. How many of us know, however, that God wants to bless us so much more than we can imagine as we allow Him more and more into our lives. The next day, quite spontaneously, the lady also found out that she was free from all her financial debt, which had been a four figure number!

- **Warning and strategy.** As in the example at the beginning of this chapter of the spiritual map of our city, "Surely the Sovereign Lord does nothing without revealing his plan to his servants the prophets," (Amos 3:7).
- **Breakthrough.** Here are a couple of typical stories received from our latest meeting whilst I was writing this section of the book:

"Firstly, it was AMAZING! Particularly during the bit where X and Y were waving the flags and celebrating the gifts of those who walked through. When walking through the flags, Holy Spirit flooded my whole body and I felt such a freedom that I haven't felt in ages. During the soaking time at SOL, the presence of God was so tangible. I saw a cross drawn over me and the lines turned to fire and Holy Spirit pressed into my heart and restarted it. God said to me 'You are called, you are chosen, rise up' and I started to cry as I

could feel and see the things which had bound me being lifted and removed from me. God is so good!"

"I couldn't have been more surprised at the deep level of healing that I received that evening. Having thought I had dealt with many issues, I am so grateful for the Holy Spirit's perception that there were deep rooted wounds. I have never seen or experienced anything like that before, but am so grateful for it. I am living in freedom today. At the beginning of the meeting I had asked to be unfettered, unchained. By the end of it I was! The very next day I felt in a different place entirely – with almost a new level of clarity and authority over my life – and in my roles in both personal and work experiences."

In our experience, the more we go beyond of the walls of the Church into our community and marketplace, the more commonplace is the release of God's grace, love, signs and wonders.

Kris Vallotton of Bethel Church, Redding, prophesied recently that the Lord is transitioning his body from a "Bethesda Pool" to an "Ezekiel river". The pool of Bethesda represents a static place for people to receive healing, while the Ezekiel river starts at the temple and flows into the marketplace (Ezekiel 47).

❝ Many Christians are already hearing God's voice, but may not recognise it. Speakers of Life seeks to encourage and practice hearing God's voice and applying his words to bless others, inside and outside the walls of the Church. Kingdom of God come! ❞

2 Foundational Principles

In this chapter I want to look at some foundational truths that underpin the SOL ministry. We will consider the definition of prophecy, how it is rooted in the word of God, and what the Bible says about the role of a prophet or seer.

The definition of prophecy

In general, most of the available literature on the prophetic ministry agrees that, in its simplest form, prophecy is "hearing God speak and repeating what he says". The source of prophecy is, of course, crucial and must stem from our personal relationship with the living dynamic of the Trinity of God the Father, Jesus the Son, and the Holy Spirit. 2 Peter 1:21 points out that, "...prophecy never had its origin in the will of man, but men spoke from God as they were carried along by the Holy Spirit."

Revelation

All prophecy ultimately points to Jesus, our wonderful Saviour and

Lord who so extravagantly loves us (1 John 3:1). It is about helping us to know him and making him known to others. It is about carrying a testimony of Christ, borne out of a personal revelation of him. As Revelation 19:10 says,

"For the testimony of Jesus is the spirit of prophecy."

Prophecy may contain other elements, such as words of knowledge about current situations or information about the future, but these are of secondary importance. The main focus is always to point people towards Jesus. The true purpose of prophecy is therefore to impart/receive revelation regarding the Lordship of Christ (see Paul's comment in 1 Corinthians 12:3: "No one can say 'Jesus is Lord,' except by the Holy Spirit"). Knowledge is not our primary goal. Prophetic words are signposts to the One who is the answer. In SOL, whether we are in a church setting, on the streets, community treasure hunting, or interpreting dreams at spiritual/psychic fayres, we are seeking to point people to Jesus.

Kris Vallotton helpfully describes prophecy in terms of "foretelling" and "forth telling". Foretelling is knowing the future (Acts 11:28) and forth telling is "causing" the future – in other words, speaking it into being (Ezekiel 37:1-10). Kris makes the distinction between the word of knowledge – the revelation of a fact about which we had no prior knowledge that concerns the past or the present, and which has no future element – and "pure prophecy" which is about the future.

This, of course, does not mean that a prophetic utterance cannot include an element of the word of knowledge. In fact, Holy Spirit will often use this gift to grab a person's attention, highlighting some piece of information no one else but the recipient (and God) could know, before the foretelling/forth telling begins. A SOL member's story highlights this:

"I asked God if there was anything he wanted to say to me and he told me that a good friend (who was not a Christian) had been to visit a fortune teller and, as a result, their marriage was experiencing difficulties. I carefully shared this word of knowledge with the couple at an appropriate time, which certainly got their attention as it was true! They then gave me permission to prophetically bless their marriage and break the curse in the name of Jesus."

Confirmation

Prophecy often confirms, or brings into focus, the way in which the Holy Spirit is already leading us (Greg Haslam, Moving in the Prophetic, Monarch). Often, the role of the prophet is to confirm to a person, that which God has already spoken to them.

Love, love, love

1 Corinthians 14:3 tells us that, "...the one who prophesies speaks to people for their strengthening, encouraging and comfort." It is clear that this is something more than merely speaking encouraging, kind words with good intentions (the product of human wisdom). It is a supernatural strengthening and impartation of encouragement and comfort, delivered from the throne room of Heaven from a loving God whose eye is upon us 24/7 and who is always in a good mood! Kris Vallotton writes that the "primary purpose of prophecy is not to direct or correct, but to encourage the church."

Prophecy is a gift

Prophecy is one of the nine gifts of the Holy Spirit listed in 1 Corinthians 12:4-11. We are urged to, "eagerly desire spiritual gifts, especially the gift of prophecy." Notice that Paul's dialogue regarding spiritual gifts appears in the context of verse 7: "the manifestation of the Spirit is given for the common good" and he continues by pointing out, "Love bears all things, believes all things, hopes all things, endures all things" (1 Corinthians 13:7).

As with all of the spiritual gifts, moving in the prophetic is not necessarily a sign of Christian maturity and does not make someone a "super" Christian or "more spiritual" than others. Kris Vallotton points out that, "Prophecy is a gift, not an award. We didn't earn it, we received it by asking. This means that very gifted people are not necessarily mature Christians ... the gifts of the Spirit do not validate our walk with God. It is the fruit of the Spirit that is developed as a person matures in Christ" (Galatians 5:22-23).

Knowing that a) the gifts God gives us are for the benefit of others, b) that we must minister them from a heart of love, and c) that possessing and using the gifts does not make us mature or any better than anyone else, should serve to keep us both humble and dependent on Father God. We all need to keep on being filled with the Holy Spirit, since he provides the power (dunamis in Greek, from which we get the word "dynamite") behind the gifts (Acts 1:8). The process of being filled to overflowing with the Holy Spirit is a continuous process. Ephesians 5:18 uses the present continuous tense to encourage us to be "continually filled".

The 3 key prophetic components:
Revelation, Interpretation and Application

The overwhelming view from prophetic literature is that each prophetic word comprises three different components, namely Revelation, Interpretation and Application. Let's look at each of these in turn.

Revelation

The first component of the prophetic word is the information that is revealed to us by God. It is information that we do not have knowledge of, naturally speaking – typically things that we could not know about a person, situation or event unless God revealed it to us supernaturally. If we want to hear from God and live a prophetic lifestyle, a good first step is simply to ask the Lord to show us things. For example, to give us his insights into a specific situation so that we can begin to pray in line with his will for it.

Interpretation

The second part of the prophetic word is interpretation. It gives understanding to what the revelation means. If we see something in the Spirit, but don't understand it, we are to ask the Lord for understanding.

Application

This third component of the prophetic word is the response to parts one and two. In other words, how we implement, respond to or utilise the revelation and interpretation God gives us. Again, we ask the Lord what to do with this. Many times, the application (and indeed the interpretation) is not the job of the person who receives and imparts the revelation. Often the role of the prophet is simply to relay revelation and this will invariably "connect" with the recipient who will be able to interpret and apply the word to their situation.

As Paul points out in 1 Corinthians 13:12, at present we see "through a glass, dimly". In other words, we don't always get all three components of the prophetic word on our own. In SOL our aim is to work in teams and, besides the fact that this means we have good accountability, it means that one person doesn't have to have the whole picture.

Understanding this principle should help us to open our mouths and speak words of life to others – trusting that God will give them the full picture, even if we don't have it all. One thing we can be sure of is that if we say nothing, then it is guaranteed that nothing will happen! As Steve Thompson puts it, "A prophetic word that is not given cannot minister to anyone." If we follow the way of love and open our mouths within the parameters of strengthening, encouraging and comforting, however, then the minimum benefit is that the person will know that God loves them, since you have made yourself vulnerable to step into a place of potential embarrassment with the sole motive of blessing them. That's already a win!

Additional benefits of prophecy

In addition to strengthening, encouraging and comforting, there are other benefits to prophecy which include:

- Use in prayer ministry and counselling
- Use in teaching
- For correction and warning
- To reveal identity and release destiny
- Spiritual warfare
- To provide vision and direction
- Prayer and intercession
- Evangelism (the testimony of Jesus is the spirit of prophecy (Revelation 19:10)

Rooted in the word of God

It is vital to understand that the prophetic word always compliments and never competes with or replaces the word of God, the Bible. We are meant to feed on God's written word every day. Revelatory gifting provides the icing on the cake, but it's not the main course. A firm grounding in God's word will ensure that we don't become "prophecy junkies". In other words, relying on prophetic words from others for our direction in life and becoming dependent on their revelation, rather than depending solely on Jesus, the lover of our soul.

All revelatory ministry is built upon the foundation of the word of God. As Paul wrote to Timothy,

"All Scripture is God-breathed and is useful for teaching, rebuking, correcting and training in righteousness, so that the servant of God may be thoroughly equipped for every good work." (2 Timothy 3:16-17)

However we desire to be used by God – treasure hunting, prophecy on the streets etc – we must be rooted in his word. For the last 20 years I have read the Bible from cover to cover every year, as I feed daily on the life of the word of God. What we feed on is ultimately what will come out of us if someone prods us. As someone said, "Rubbish in, rubbish out". How about, "Life in, life out"? If we are full of God's word, then it is likely we will react to people and situations by speaking his supernatural, life-giving words and thus see the spiritual atmosphere change. It is important that God's word finds a home in us and is not just an occasional visitor. As Colossians 3:16 says:

"Let the word of Christ dwell in you richly in all wisdom, teaching and admonishing one another in psalms and hymns and spiritual songs, singing with grace in your hearts to the Lord."

Prophets and Seers

Derek Prince describes the gift of prophecy as the supernaturally imparted ability to hear the voice of the Holy Sprit and speak God's mind or counsel. In the New Testament only two words are used for prophecy: the Greek words propheteia and prophetikos – the most common of which is propheteia. Dick Iverson explains that propheteia means, "speaking forth the mind and counsel of God".

Kenneth Hagin articulates the Greek in a similar way: to speak to another on behalf of God; to be a spokesperson.

Hagin writes that the Hebrew word for prophecy means to flow forth or bubble up like a fountain. This Hebrew word, nabi or nahbi, not only describes the inner "bubbling up" of the words of God, leading us to speak them out, but also describes the pictures of both a seed and a tent. In other words, the prophetic word literally sows seeds (life) into someone's tent (their life or sphere of influence). Paula Price expands this idea further in The Prophet's Handbook, explaining that, unlike the Greek perception of the prophetic, the Hebrews saw prophecy as "much more than a simple predictor. For them the ministry had a power-wielding influence that affected destiny and dramatically impacted the world around them."

What about seers? What are they and why does the Bible distinguish between them and prophets? Asaph and Gad are described as seers in David's court (2 Chronicles 29:30; 2 Samuel 24:11-12), in contrast to Nathan who is denoted a prophet in the court (2 Samuel 7:2-5).

In 1 Chronicles 29:29 we read all three of the Old Testament definitions of prophet and seer in one verse:

"As for the events of King David's reign, from beginning to end, they are written in the records of Samuel the seer [ra'ah], the records of Nathan the prophet [nahbi/nabi] and the records of Gad the seer [chozeh]".

The Old Testament uses a different word – ra'ah – to describe a seer. It means to see, gaze, look upon, perceive. Occasionally the Bible also uses the word chozeh, which refers to the beholder of a vision, a gazer or stargazer. Paula Price describes the seer as a type of prophet who "regularly peers into the other [spiritual] world."

Again, these rich Hebrew words also encapsulate the idea of a tent. Ra'ah and chozeh can refer to a tent wall and also a cutting tool. Jim Goll refers to this in his book The Seer, showing how the prophetic can cut through or pierce the divide between the physical and spiritual realms. A great example of this is illustrated in 2 Kings 6:15-17 where the Lord opens the eyes of Elisha's servant, enabling him to see into the spiritual realm and perceive the heavenly help that is always available to us.

"When the servant of the man of God got up and went out early the next morning, an army with horses and chariots had surrounded the city. 'Oh no, my lord! What shall we do?' the servant asked. 'Don't be afraid,' the prophet answered. 'Those who are with us are more than those who are with them.' And Elisha prayed, 'Open his eyes, Lord, so that he may see.' Then the Lord opened the servant's eyes, and he looked and saw the hills full of horses and chariots of fire all around Elisha."

What is the difference between a prophet and a seer?

Jim Goll writes that all true seers are prophets, but not all prophets are seers. Prophets are communicative (speaking), whereas seers are receptive (beholding, gazing). The nabi prophet is often spontaneous and activated by faith, whereas the ra'ah seer is more dependent upon the manifested presence of God.

A person with a seer-type prophetic gift will often "see" things in the Spirit, such as details of an event before it happens, or things about a person before they meet them – where they will sit at a meeting, their name, their appearance and so on.

Paula Price points out that prophets will often communicate by saying, "The Lord is saying...", whereas seers will describe what they are seeing with words such as, "The Lord is showing me..." or "I can see..." Although it is not exclusive to seers, they tend to see visions regularly and will often see angels or demons in the spiritual realm. Such a gift does not, however, always guarantee that others will be "strengthened, encouraged and comforted", so it is important that prophets and seers work together in teams to be effective. They also need to work in tandem to help others understand and develop their own prophetic gifts. As Jonathan Welton writes in his book, The School of Seers, prophets and seers can work together to teach others to receive revelation in the way they receive it.

Are there seers in the New Testament?

In the Israel of the Old Testament, if someone went to inquire of God, they would say, "Come, let us go to the seer." Over time, the Hebrew terms for prophet were "merged" and taken to mean the same thing. I am a molecular biologist by profession, but other colleagues have different disciplines, such as cell biologists, nanobioligists and microbiologists. For the convenience of the non-expert, we are all "biologists". Similarly, in the New Testament, prophets and seers still function, but for convenience they are both described by the catch-all "prophet".

Jonathan Welton identifies New Testament seers as those who have the gift of spiritual insight, such as discerning of spirits (1 Corinthians 12). Seers are those who may perceive the presence of the angelic, for instance. Francis Frangipane in his book Spiritual Discernment and the Mind of Christ, writes that, "Spiritual discernment is the grace to see into the unseen realm, to perceive the realm of the spirit … and this is not a faculty of our minds."

Watch and pray

In the New Testament Jesus tells us to watch and pray. This encourages us not only to pray, but also to dwell in the "seer" realm. In other words, to watch with the eyes of our heart. God asked Jeremiah, "What do you see?" when referring to the branch of an almond tree (Jeremiah 1:11-12) and he was commended for seeing correctly. The literal meaning of "almond" is to watch or wake. It was a useful metaphor since in Israel, at that time, the almond tree was the first to wake from the sleep of winter (Matthew Henry's commentary). Further scriptures speak of being in the right position (standing in the council of the Lord or being stationed on the ramparts) at the right time to see and hear from God and to communicate this in different ways (Jeremiah 23:18-22 and Habakkuk 2:1).

Founded on love; delivered in love

The first five words of the 1 Corinthians 14 passage create the context out of which prophecy is to be delivered. They say, "Follow the way of love". Prophecy is about love, love, love! If we follow the way of love, this makes it easy to strengthen, encourage and comfort; to deliver prophetic messages in a way that honours, blesses, frees and wants the very best for the recipient.

Used in its proper context, prophecy is all about speaking life. What does this look like in practice? It means mining for the gold in people that exists beneath the surface, rather than focusing on the more apparent dirt. God loves to speak to people in terms of who they can become, in him, in the future. Therefore prophecy is often about uncovering the hidden treasure in people and articulating it to them. If we see, discern or hear something negative about a person we are ministering to, then rather than speak negatively over them, we should ask Holy Spirit for the answer to their problem. In this way we will remain true to the principle of strengthening, encouraging and comforting, and the speaking of life will help the person to receive grace from God to solve their problem. Another way of looking at this is to speak out and pray the opposite to the problem. If we discern fear, then we speak out the love of God to expel the fear (1 John 4:18).

Overcoming barriers

If we follow "the way of love", God will use our prophetic words to disarm situations and pierce the barriers which people erect around their lives. There are numerous biblical examples. In John 1:35-51 we see sceptical Nathanael's defences pierced by Jesus' revelatory words as he speaks to the hidden treasure in him. Then in John 4:7-26 we see Jesus' disarm the Samaritan woman at the well as he speaks prophetically about her life with love and grace. There were numerous barriers to her hearing and receiving God's message of life to her:

- She was a woman and Jesus was a single man. It was culturally unacceptable for them to be conversing in public
- She was deceitful, having withheld the truth
- She and Jesus were from different ethnic groups which, historically, had nothing to do with one another
- She worshipped false gods
- She was an adulteress living an immoral life

Jesus' words of life cut through all of the spiritual, cultural and social barriers and touched her heart. Her response was to receive revelation of the fact that he was not only a prophet, but the promised Messiah.

This should give us a great deal of encouragement. We may see all kinds of barriers in the lives of others that, to our understanding, make it very hard for them to receive God's word in their life. By focusing on the barriers we can almost give up before we've started. We shouldn't underestimate the power of the life of Jesus in us, expressed to others through our words. God's words of life can penetrate any barrier. Consider, for examples, the following story from a SOL member:

"God challenged me to pray for one of my work colleagues. One night, He woke me at 3.00am with a very clear picture of an older female colleague who was walking around her kitchen table. She then took a seat opposite her husband with a cup of hot chocolate. They seemed distressed. I prayed for about an hour and a half that the presence of God would be with them and comfort them. The next day, God challenged me to share the picture with the lady. This was a big barrier to me and my ego. My initial thought was, 'I can't do that!' Eventually, I plucked up the courage to tell her the following day.

After I relayed the details of what I'd seen to her, she looked at me in shock and told me that at exactly that time in the morning she had received a phone call to say that her father had been taken ill. She confirmed the exact details from the picture, even down to the hot chocolate in the kitchen. She asked how I had known about it, so I told her that God cared for her and that she was very loved by and special to him — so much so that he had woken me up to pray for her. I'm glad I didn't give up and not tell her."

God's perspective – seeing what he sees

As Rick Joyner points out, every true prophet must pass the Ezekiel 37 dry bones test. What do we see in the present valley of dry bones? Without a vision from heaven we can see only death. God, however, can see in even the driest of bones an amazing army and instructs us to speak out his life. We speak life into the lives of others until they become what God has called them to be. We urge them to step into their destiny and calling. God says, "You see dry bones. I see an army." Seeing things from God's perspective is always the best!

How do you perceive the "dry bones" situation that exists in your daily life right now? In Ezekiel 37:4-5 God encouraged Ezekiel to,

"Prophesy to these bones and say to them, 'Dry bones, hear the word of the Lord ... I will make breath enter you, and you will come to life!'"

The "before" and "after" effects of God releasing His breath into a situation look very different. Before, life looks impossible. Afterwards, life abounds and our situation has been unrecognisably transformed. God can take the driest of bones, the deadest of situations, and utterly turn them around. The prophetic word from God (spoken through Ezekiel or whichever agent he so chooses) is power (dunamis). His word, "will not return to me empty, but will accomplish what I desire and achieve the purpose for which I sent it" (Isaiah 55:11).

Amazing breakthroughs happen when we partner with God. As we speak and release God's words of life over individuals and circumstances, the miraculous happens. Do we need any more convincing to become a speaker of life? As Romans 4:17 declares,

"God gives life to the dead and calls things that are not as though they were."

Let's each one of us practice hearing what God is saying, see what God is seeing, and speak them out. There is a desperate need to do this. We all have friends, relatives, colleagues, even strangers, who we encounter in our daily lives who need bread from heaven. Our human wisdom has little or nothing to offer them. But Jesus wants to freely give us knowledge, wisdom, prophetic insight and discernment that will pierce the darkness in their lives. And he does so extravagantly and without limit, as he expresses the vast, expansive love of a Heavenly Daddy who desires to call them sons and daughters of the Living God, because that is what he sees in them!

3 Guiding Principles

So far we have discussed the concept of speaking life to others and looked at the definition and aims of prophecy. Now we turn our attention to some practical matters. Frequently, people ask me how to hear God more clearly and how they can receive/process revelation. We'll look at those issues in this chapter.

Tuning into God

God's heart is to speak to us. He loves to communicate with his children! Frequently, however, we allow the noise of life to obscure what he is saying, and so we need to be intentional about tuning into him.

Learn to identify his voice

Imagine yourself in a large, crowded room. There are many people talking and there is also some music playing in the background. On the far side of the room your young child falls over, bumps themselves and cries out – or your spouse/best friend laughs out loud. To anyone these sounds are just part of the general background noise, but your ear is tuned to these voices and you pick them up instantly, even above the general hubbub.

In the same way Jesus invites us to become familiar with his voice. John 10:4 says, "his sheep follow him because they know his voice." The more time we spend with him (we'll explore this more in Ch4 on soaking), the more easily we will recognise his voice – and be able to identify it above the competing noise that is part of our daily lives.

The context of John 10:4 is of the Great Shepherd leading his sheep to safe pasture. What a promise! What are we waiting for? Next time we hear his voice we must respond to it and not harden our hearts (Hebrews 4:7), since his voice can accomplish amazing things (Psalm 29).

Make Jesus your focus

When I was learning to windsurf, the best piece of advice I received was to take my eyes off the front end of the sailboard and lift my head to focus on where I wanted to go. I found that I did indeed head in the direction I wanted to go, got there in a straight line, and did so much quicker too!

Proverbs 4:25 says,

"Let your eyes look straight ahead; fix your gaze directly before you." Hebrews 12:2 tells us that there is only one on whom we should focus our attention: "Let us fix our eyes on Jesus, the author and perfector of our faith, who for the joy set before him endured the cross, scorning its shame, and sat down at the right hand of the throne of God."

We are that joy set before him! As we set our gaze and focus on him, the eternal king, it allows us to get a grip on heavenly realities. As 2 Corinthians 4:18 says, "We fix our eyes not on what is seen, but on what is unseen, since what is seen is temporary, but what is unseen is eternal."

In our daily lives, we can often tell what people are feasting upon with their eyes (books, TV, the Internet) by what they talk about and how they say it. As we focus our eyes on the eternal realm, we begin to sound like that upon which we are focussing, and the result is that we speak out the life of Jesus and the language of heaven.

This prophetic word by Jim Goll, taking from the Elijah List online resource expresses this well: "My precious child, follow me. Look up at me and you will see where I am going. You cannot follow what you cannot see. When you look down at your feet in pain or in sorrow you lose sight of where I am walking – you lose sight of me. So give me those things that drag your gaze downwards. I am quickening the pace of your journey and want to take you higher. Fix your eyes on me and see where I am going."

Learn to perceive

The more time we spend in God's presence, listening and tuning into his voice, the more our spiritual sensitivity will increase. Many Christians are already hearing God's voice, but may not perceive it.

God wants to draw us closer to him and speak to us. Until we sharpen our perception he may do that in unusual ways in order to catch our attention. We must also remember that God cannot be confined or put in a box – he doesn't work according to predictable formulas, much as we would like him to! Jesus comes and speaks to us in different forms. After his resurrection, for example, even some of his closest disciples had trouble recognising him because he appeared different to them (Mark 16:12). So a key to recognising his voice is to perceive what he is doing, not rely on a set form or pattern for recognising him.

God can be unpredictable and use different means and methods precisely so that we have to remain utterly dependent upon him. He combats our tendency to become rigid and inflexible. He wants us to remain fresh and responsive; to avoid becoming like the old wineskin that can no longer receive and contain the new wine (Luke 5:37-39). Scripture reveals that God has always been this way:

"For God does speak – now one way, now another though no one perceives it." (Job 33:14)

"See, I am doing a new thing! Now it springs up; do you not perceive it?" (Isaiah 43:19)

When we perceive what God is saying and doing we can appropriate it in our lives and the situations in which we find ourselves. In his book When Heaven Invades Earth, Bill Johnson writes, "Look up and see: My Glory arises above you, it is ever so near. My Glory arises above you, so pull it down, pull it down..." Just as Jesus encouraged us to pray in the Lord's prayer that we would see heaven on earth, so daily we need to focus on and perceive what God is saying from heaven, so that we can "pull it down" into our circumstances. We can "pull down heaven" into our relationships and see restoration. We can pull it down and see hard hearts melt; pull it down and see salvation. This is a new day and a new season!

How do we receive the revelation?

In the previous chapter we saw that the three key components of prophecy are revelation, interpretation and application. First things first, how do we receive revelation? There are various examples list below, but first it is important to grasp something of the nature of supernatural revelation. We may not fully understand the communication we receive from heaven, and the revelation we share may not immediately mean something to the person we share it with until they process it later. It is therefore very important to speak out and then give that person the space and time to weigh what you believe God is saying to them.

Don't begin speculating on the possible interpretation and meaning. It is a common mistake to do so and one that tends to cloud the waters of prophetic interpretation. It is understandable, due to our eagerness to help and be part of the answer to someone's problem, be we need to trust God. We can be confident to deliver only that which God gives us, because he is big enough and kind enough to work it out in that person's life at the right time.

Ways in which God imparts revelation to us

Since we know that, "God does speak – now one way, now another" (Job 33: 14), what does it look like? This is not an exhaustive list, but includes many of the common and well-documented examples.

1. Impressions. This is the most common way in which we receive revelation from God. Rick Joyner writes, "These are general revelations that we put into our own words" and can include a picture, an impression of pain, or a phrase or scripture. These impressions can also be subtle, almost like the sense of a butterfly briefly resting on our arm before taking off again as God speaks to us in a still small voice from within our spirit as a passing thought or sudden impression. The still small voice is illustrated in first Kings where God is in the gentle blowing and not the strong wind, earthquake or fire (1 Kings 19:11-13)."

2. Scriptures. The Lord often speaks to us in our daily readings of the Bible as a verse suddenly leaps off the page at us. The Bible is the God-breathed word (2 Timothy 3:16-17). Let's value it and read it expecting God to speak and "life" to leap at us from the page.

3. Signs and Wonders. The Bible is replete with examples, such as Gideon to whom God gives a miraculous sign in Judges 6:17-21.

There are numerous other examples!

4. Our natural senses. Sometimes God will enable us to perceive him at work using our natural senses, such as smell. An example from a SOL members illustrates this.

"At the end of preaching at one of the CTF satellite churches in Toronto I could smell freshly baked bread. The Lord gave me the prophetic word that people would come to the church knowing there is 'bread in the house'. I used the well known passage in Ruth chapter 1 about the end of the famine in Bethlehem, with the added significance that Bethlehem means 'House of Bread'. I gave this prophetic word thinking in my mind about 'spiritual bread' in the house, but the Lord often uses an example in the natural to illustrate the spiritual. On my next visit to the church, a year later, I discovered that the Sunday following the prophetic word a bakery spontaneously asked the pastors whether they could utilise spare baskets of fresh bread on a Sunday morning, which they duly delivered every week. Bread in the house, indeed!"

5. Interpretation of Tongues. See 1 Corinthians 12:8-10.

6. Discernment/distinguishing of spirits. Sometimes we may be sitting next to a person and God enables us to "pick up" that which is spiritually influencing them. For example, if we are in close proximity to a person gripped by the spirit of fear, we may suddenly sense fear or become confused. God allows us insight into situations by sensing such external influences in the Spirit.

7. Visions. Frequently God has revealed things to his servants in visions of differing types. These may be internal visions seen with the eyes of the heart (Ephesians 1:18) or open visions that are more like watching a movie on a screen in front of your eyes (such as Cornelius in Acts 10:30, for example).

8. Trances. Trances are similar to visions, except that the person is completely unaware of their surroundings (e.g. when Peter fell into a trance in Acts 10:9-11). Rick Joyner describes a trance as like having a dream whilst you are awake. John's revelation on Patmos is an example, as well as Paul describing how he was caught up to the "third heaven" in 2 Corinthians 12:2-4).

9. Dreams. There are many biblical examples, but chapter 6 of this book is dedicated to dreams and dream interpretation.

10. Translation in the Spirit. In Revelation 4:1 (and later in 11:12) we read the call to "come up here". Many prophetic writers agree that here John was temporarily "translated" into another place to experience the spiritual realities in heaven. It is no surprise, therefore, that John wrote 1 John 1-3 after these "seer type" experiences, having been influenced strongly by the light and love of his heavenly encounter. God exists and operates outside of time, so it should not be surprising to hear stories today of Christians being "translated" in the Spirit to "witness" an event or conversation many miles away or in another country. We see examples of this in the Bible, such as Ezekiel 43:5; John 1:48; 2 Kings 6:8-23; 2 Kings 5;26. When this has occurred with SOL members, they have had the opportunity to confirm and verify the experience by contacting the visited people to bless them with the heavenly insight they received. One SOL member reports,

"I was woken up with a vivid image of my church leaders being in trouble, spinning round and round in a car crash and I fervently prayed for heavenly protection. At that time it didn't make sense, as my leaders had not experienced anything like this, but exactly one year later to the day they were in a dramatic car accident with the car spinning round and round and they called out and were aware of amazing heavenly protection which surprised even the rescue

workers. My prayer exactly one year earlier was perfect timing in God's spiritual realm."

11. Creation. God can and does speak to us through the natural world around us. Romans 1:20 sums this up well: "For since the creation of the world God's invisible qualities—his eternal power and divine nature—have been clearly seen, being understood from what has been made, so that people are without excuse."

12. Audible voice. Occasionally we may hear God speak to us in an audible voice. This is different to hearing his voice inwardly in our spirits and is an awesome thing (Psalm 29).

13. Correlation of natural and spiritual events. In 1 Chronicles 12:32 the sons of Issachar are described as those who understood the signs of the times. Sometimes God will point to spiritual realities by relating them to natural events. For example, one SOL member writes,

"I was in a meeting at the Catch the Fire church in Toronto, looking at the speaker on stage who was Chief Kenny Blacksmith from the Cree nation. He was speaking about revival returning to Canada. In the Spirit I saw a river flowing out of his mouth with salmon leaping in the fast flowing water. The next day, the headline front page news in one of the main Toronto newspapers revealed that dramatic numbers of salmon had returned to a significant Canadian river for the first time!"

Similarly, Numbers 17:2-8 describes the blossoming of Aaron's staff which mirrored the spiritual confirmation of Moses' and Aaron's authority in Israel's journey and history.

14. Plays on words, puns, clothing. God is an endlessly creative

God who will speak to us in any number of ways. The important thing is we allow him to speak in any way he chooses, and not get stuck in a pattern thinking, "It only happens this way." Sometimes revelation will come in the form of a play on words that we see somewhere, as writing on an item of clothing, on a designer label etc. Jeremiah 1:11-12 is a good example. God asks Jeremiah, "What do you see?" He replies,

"I see the branch of an almond tree, I replied. The Lord said to me, 'You have seen correctly, for I am watching to see that my word is fulfilled.'"

At first reading this seems a little curious. How does God's word being fulfilled relate to an almond tree? Steve Thompson and other commentators explain that an examination of the Hebrew reveals a play on words. Jeremiah saw a shawkade which means "almond tree". In his reply the Lord says, "You have seen correctly, for I will shawkad... (a one letter difference), which in Hebrew means "watch over my word to perform it". God uses the similarity of the words to encourage Jeremiah that he is watching at all times to ensure that his word is fulfilled and does not return void.

15. Angels. Kris Vallotton writes that angels are another way in which God speaks to his servants and this is evidenced many times in the New Testament (Acts 8:26, Acts 12:6-7, for example). Angels are "ministering spirits sent to serve those will inherit salvation" (Hebrews 1:14), so we should expect to experience, see or be aware of this angelic help as we ask the Lord for help. Angels are under the Lord's command and are dispatched in the way and manner that is of most help to us. Martin Luther the German reformer wrote that, "an angel is a spiritual creature created by God for the service of Christendom and of the church." If the Lord has gone to the trouble of sending help in the form of angels, it would be at best impolite not to receive this help or be looking out for it.

What kind of angelic intervention should we expect? One story from a SOL member may help in this regard:

"I had been asking God to see his heavenly help and felt that my mind was getting in the way of this. So at the beginning of the service that Sunday I just gave God my mind for him to transform it (Romans 12:2). I was at Bethel Church, Redding, which is known for having many angelic encounters. Half way through the worship I began to see in the spirit that there were five angels around me. One was inches away, looking me in the eyes and combing oil through my hair. Two more were either side of my head, blowing trumpets into my ears (like a herald). The fourth was fitting my feet with shoes of peace (Ephesians 6) and the final angel was providing me with a belt (of truth, Ephesians 6) and a robe (symbolising righteousness, Isaiah 61:10).

This was such a vivid experience that I remember thinking, 'Either I am having a nervous breakdown or this is really happening.' I remember asking God, 'If this is of you, please could you confirm it? Literally a few minutes later two senior ministry leaders came up to me and said, 'Sorry for disturbing you in worship, but we have been watching you for the last ten minutes. Do you know that there are five angels around you? One combing oil through your hair, two with trumpets, one with a robe and belt and other with shoes for your feet.' Confirmation indeed!"

The early church was very familiar with angelic appearances and help. For example, in Acts 12 we read of Peter being released from prison and going to the believers who were praying for him behind closed doors. It was easier for them to believe that the man knocking at the door of the room where they were praying was Peter's angel rather than Peter himself.

It goes without saying that, following the example of the Church in the Bible, all the glory always goes to God, not to his angels and we do not worship angels, we always worship Jesus (Hebrews 1 and 2). Jesus must always remain preeminent, but out of this context we can look forward to receiving heavenly help dispatched by God whenever we need it.

More about angels

The word "angel" or "angels" appears 300 times in the Bible and there are 104 recorded angelic encounters. Although we may have read or experienced quite a lot about angels and their presence, here is a brief, one-stop checklist of the fundamental facts.

• Angels may or may not have wings. Those that do may have a different numbers of wings, e.g. four wings (Cherubim, Ezekiel 1 and 10) or six wings (Seraphim, Ch6:2-3). Sometimes it is useful to know these facts as shown in the account from a SOL member while visiting a church in Fulham, London. "During the last worship song I noticed two angels with six wings each (I knew they were seraphim) appear either side of the lead pastor who was standing at the front ready to preach. Afterwards I mustered enough courage to tell him the story, at which point he began to smile one of those ear-to-ear smiles. He was so happy and encouraged as he then explained that during the last worship song he asked God specifically for seraphim either side of him to help him with his message that morning. He had never previously done this and was therefore greatly encouraged to do so again in the future."

• As well as being bright in appearance (Ezekiel and Revelation) they may also have the appearance of people from various cultures and ethnic origins (Genesis 19, Hebrews 13:2: "Do not neglect to show hospitality to strangers for by this some have entertained angels without knowing it.")

- Angels speak languages known and unknown to us (1 Corinthians 13:1) and they also worship and proclaim (with trumpets etc; Revelation 8:2; 1 Thessalonians 4:16). In this context, here are a few accounts of the many angelic encounters which occur at our regular monthly SOL meetings:

"During an extended period of silence in the meeting I was waiting on God when I and others in the room distinctly heard heavenly singing."

In addition, a lady who has a sharp, established, prophetic edge wrote about that same night: "I was washing my hands in the bathroom and I heard an almighty cheer. I thought, 'What am I missing?' As I came back into the room, one of the pastors was at the door so I asked what everyone was cheering for. He told me, 'They weren't!' but I heard that cheer with my natural ears." We quickly realised that it was the heavenly hosts cheering and applauding us for what was happening that evening as we met in the unity of the Holy Spirit in the name of Jesus.

- Angelic appearances can be associated with wind and fire. Hebrew 1:7 and Psalm 104:4 say, "He makes his angels winds, his servants flames of fire." Sometimes people have been made aware of the presence of angels when a breeze or wind passes by in a place where there is no natural breeze. Others have experienced the presence of an intense heat. Here is an account from a SOL team who were invited to go to Sheffield, UK, to prophesy over the city:

"As we stood on a hill overlooking Sheffield, we noticed several large dormant angels in strategic places over the city. We felt

prompted to activate the angels and in accordance with the Ezekiel 37 scripture, to form a line and blow on the dry bones of the city. We blew and waited. It was a calm day with no wind. Literally thirty seconds later, a strong wind came from nowhere and knocked us all off our feet. The whole team ended up falling backwards to the grassy ground."

• Some of the main orders of angels are Archangels (meaning covering angels who are over other angels. See Jude 9 and the anointed angel who covers that is described in Ezekiel 28:13-16). At the top level there are angels such as Gabriel and Michael and the fallen Lucifer. Then we have Cherubim (Ezekiel 10 and Genesis 3) and Seraphim, which means the burning ones (Isaiah 6:3) and who are often associated with holiness. Jim Goll and others remark that there is often a sense of the smell of burning coal or charcoal when seraphim are around. A story from a SOL member concurs with this:

"I was teaching on holiness during a prophetic workshop in the Catch the Fire church, Toronto. Suddenly I and about eight others could simultaneously smell burning charcoal and there was an increased sense of the angelic presence. We checked that nothing was on fire in the building and concluded that seraphim had come to help with the ministry, which of course was all about holiness."

We need all the help we can get to stay the course of the highway of holiness described in Isaiah 35:1-10. This is because the potential fruit is so amazing, such as restoration (v2, 7), healing and strength (v4), safety and protection (v9), and the gladness and joy that will overtake us (v10) in the same way as we read in Deuteronomy 28 and Psalm 23.

• As Jim Goll describes in his book Angelic Encounters, there are other categories of angels in the vast company of heaven including:
  • The angel of the Lord (Psalm 34:7)
  • Angels assigned to churches (Revelation 1:20)
  • Guardian angels (Matthew 18:2-3,10; Acts 12:13-15)
  • Angels of great authority (Revelation 18:1-2), sometimes referred to as territorial angels, examples of which were documented by the Celtic Christians, in particular St Cuthbert (see Fire of the North by David Adam)
  • Strong angels (Revelation 10:1-3 and 18:21)

Goll summarises that the tasks assigned to angels fall into two major categories, namely directive and protective. Directive examples are angels releasing dreams, revelation and understanding (helping Mary, Joseph and Daniel, for example); delivering God's messages (Luke 1:19-20); imparting strength (Genesis 16) and relaying God's guidance (Numbers 22:31-35). Examples of protection are the guardian role (Matthew 18:10); bringing deliverance (Psalm 34:7) and releasing healing (John 5:2-4). In the context of healing many revival leaders take note of what the angels are doing and simply announce it. For example, during many SOL meetings, those who can see angels (with their spiritual eyes or natural eyes) simply point out that, for instance, the timing is right for healing backs if they see angels attending to people's backs in the gathering. A SOL member who was leading a meeting for Christians working at the United Nations in New York writes,

"I noticed that many angels were in the room attending to people's knees. I simply announced that God wanted to heal knees and for people to receive this. Many people responded and many knees were completely healed. What was amazing was that those who

had bad knees who came into the meeting late and did not hear the
healing call were also healed – some of them before they had time
to take their seat!"

In the natural we notice when someone brings a helpful or unhelpful presence into a room (such as a peaceful influence, a moody/angry influence etc) and this is often dictated by where they have come from and what they have been doing. Similarly, Jim Goll writes that, "Angels who spend much of their time before the throne of God can't help but bring God's presence to a place!" Sometimes that presence is identifiable in one of the ways mentioned above – an aroma, wind or heat – and could also be a feeling of electricity, a visible light or a "weight" (a feeling of pressure). Many of the SOL family have remarked that on occasions they have felt someone nudge or bump them, only to find there was no person close to them. They concluded that an angel was close by them. Certainly we read in both the Old and New Testament about angels ascending and descending from heaven to earth carrying the glory of God (Genesis 28:12 and John 1:51).

How to deliver prophecy

When God does speak to us and give us a word for a specific person or situation, how do we handle that? Here are some guidelines to ensure we deliver prophetic words to others following the way of love, and with both sensitivity and accountability.

1. Write it down. If you have the opportunity (i.e. God gives you a word for someone in advance of seeing them), write the word down. This really helps with the delivery of it, so that you can speak it to the person without stumbling over your words. If this method was good enough for Habakkuk and King David then it's good enough for us! (Habakkuk 2:2; 1 Chronicles 28:19).

2. Be obedient. Only say what God has given you and no more. When he stops speaking, so do you. Resist the urge to embellish upon or add to his words. Don't go on to speak out your good intentions because they lack power.

3. Speak life and follow the way of love. Remember to speak in love. Pronounce "life" not "death" over people. If you sense confusion, speak out clarity; if you sense fear, speak peace. Speak out the love-centred opposite of the negative influences God reveals. Kris Vallotton writes that if a person is "struggling with pornography, the Holy Spirit will often give us a prophetic word for them such as: 'God is calling you to a new level of purity and holiness.' In this way we have prophesied the answer without speaking about the problem and have released grace to break the bondage..."

This does not mean that the prophetic won't lead on to ministry/ counselling and result in deliverance, for instance, but observing this principle enables God to work by his grace, focussing on the "life solution" rather than the problem.

4. Use normal language and normal tone. Speak as you would normally in an everyday conversation. It is not necessary to launch into King James language or to sound like Shakespeare (unless you speak like that in everyday life of course!) Unless you are delivering a message in a noisy meeting and it's not possible to find a quiet place, it is seldom necessary to raise your voice.

5. Don't trap people by what you say or how you say it. If appropriate, smile when you prophesy. Why? Because body language is important. You want the person to feel at ease and not like they are being confronted. Then, give them room to consider, accept or reject the word. In general, the "Thus saith the Lord" type delivery does not give the recipient much room for manoeuvre. It is important to be confident in what you say, but you can say things like, "I sense the Lord wants to say" or "I believe the Lord wants to" or ask, "Does this mean anything to you?"

Rick Joyner in his book Prophetic Ministry says, "If something is truly the word of the Lord, it will accomplish his purpose without the embellishment we often tend to think prophecy needs." He continues to highlight that the goal of the prophetic is not to be spectacular, but to be effective.

If someone rejects the word immediately, for whatever reason, don't take offence and think they are rejecting you as a person. Consider Jesus, who was let down and rejected by those closest to him, yet never took offence, responding instead with love. If we find that we often feel offended, it may suggest that we are not completely dead to sin in that area of our lives. As Rick Joyner says, "It is impossible for a dead man to feel rejection." Let's take any personal issues we may have to the cross so that they can be put to death.

6. You are allowed to get it wrong. Each one of us exercising the prophetic gift is a prophet in training, which means we won't get it right all the time. The ultimate safeguard is to keep your focus on bringing glory to Jesus and following the way of love, wanting God's best for the person. If you are wrong, the worst that can happen is the person will know you are trying to bless them and express God's love for them.

7. Operate under authority. It is important that we don't become prophetic mavericks. We therefore need to operate under appropriate godly authority. Kris Vallotton states that, especially if a word is directed towards a church congregation, then it is wise to first submit it to "prophetic gatekeepers who are aware of what the Holy Spirit is doing with worship and what direction the sermon will take. These people are able to determine if a prophetic word will be fitting for a particular service." Accompanying an open microphone, free-for-all approach is the danger that the service will head off into some unwanted backwater and stem the flow of the river of life.

8. Where possible, consider working in a team. Paul counselled us to use the following model: "two or three prophets should speak, and the others should weigh carefully what is said" (1 Corinthians 14:29). Francis Frangipane writes in Spiritual Discernment and the Mind of Christ, "The admonition to minister as two or three instead of a singular individual is an important safeguard." It introduces accountability, which is always helpful. Also, we don't always get the whole picture and God delights in bringing together different parts of his body in harmony to deliver his whole message. Jesus sent out his disciples in twos and threes and promised that where two or three are gathered he is in their midst (Matthew 18:20)

9. Maintain your focus. Finally, and above all, keep your focus on Jesus and don't allow anything to muddy the waters. The enemy likes to distract us so that we shift our gaze away from the Lord, but prophets are described as the "eyes" of Christ's body (Isaiah 29:10; Luke 11:34; Job 31:1), so it is important that we keep focussed.

How to receive/test a prophetic word

We have considered how to deliver a prophetic word, but how should we receive one? And how do we know whether or not it is from God? Here are some simple tests.

1. Does it match the biblical test to strengthen, encourage and comfort?
2. Does it point to Jesus and bring glory and honour to him?
3. Does it line up with Scripture? No accurate prophetic word will contradict the teaching of the Bible, which stands alone as the plumb line against which any prophecy must be measured and judged.
4. Does it ring true and bear witness with your spirit? Does it

bring a sense of peace?

5. Does it bring you life and freedom?

Later we can ask the very practical questions,

1. Did it come true?

2. Has it borne good fruit (Luke 6:43-45)? In other words, did it bring you closer to God and deepen your relationship with him?

How to respond to/steward a prophetic word

1. First of all, we must **remember to remain open to God speaking** and not be put off by the style of delivery.

2. Secondly, **we mustn't stifle prophecy**. Rather, we are to follow the simple guidance of 1 Thessalonians 5:19-21: "Do not quench the Spirit. Do not treat prophecies with contempt but test them all; hold on to what is good..."

There are two parts to consider: to test and then to keep the good. If some of the prophetic word is wrong, but some of it is correct, keep the good and hold onto it. We don't discard the good just because one part was inaccurate. Prophets can make mistakes without being false prophets. Sometimes the mistake is simply that the prophet keeps on talking when he/she should be quiet! They may have been meant to give the revelation only, but then tried to add the interpretation or application – another good reason why prophets should work in twos or threes.

Sometimes prophets just get things plain wrong, but this does not undermine their ministry – it just shows they are human! In Acts 27:10 Paul prophesied that a sea voyage was going to be "disastrous" and would "bring great loss to ship and cargo, and to our own lives also." Later in verses 22-24 an angel corrects Paul and says there will be no loss of life – quite an important point if you were due to be a passenger on the ship!

A misinterpretation of prophecy is recorded in Acts 21:10-12 where Agabus prophesied that the Jews in Jerusalem would bind Paul and hand him over to the Gentiles. What actually happened was that the Jews were about to kill Paul when the Gentiles arrived and rescued him from the Jews, then the Gentiles bound him, not the Jews. The revelation that Agabus received was accurate, but the interpretation had a few minor details confused.

Therefore we shouldn't throw out a whole prophecy if there are a few points that are not correct or misinterpreted.

3. If a word is clearly from God, we **give thanks and take ownership of it**, acknowledging the fact that he has spoken into our life.

4. **Write it down or record it** – on a smartphone, for instance – as per Habakkuk 2:2; 1 Chronicles 28:19)

5. **Pray and ask God about it.**

6. **Ask the opinion of others you trust.** It is a good idea to share any prophetic word with those to whom you are accountable (small group leader, cell leader, church leaders (Hebrews 13:17) or trusted friends). This approach often protects us from "selective hearing". Sometimes our need can obscure some of what we hear and others who know us well can help us to keep things in perspective. This assumes that we are following biblically balanced leaders who demonstrate the fruit of the Holy Spirit and the love of Jesus in their lives.

7. **Ponder and treasure it in your heart** (Luke 2:51). With regard to sharing the word with other people, we need to do so prayerfully (Matthew 7:6). It may be that, for a time (bearing in mind the previous comment about sharing it with leaders) we are meant to ponder the meaning of the word privately. If we share the word too hastily with others, sometimes we can be greeted with simply unbelief or well meaning but off-target

feedback that causes confusion and distraction.

8. **Wait on God for further confirmation/interpretation then act on it by faith.** If the outworking of a prophetic word is clearly your responsibility (e.g. God tells you that you need to forgive a certain person), then do it. If the outworking is beyond your control, it is important that you don't strive to try and make the prophetic word come true. Remember that Abraham and Sarah tried to help God in the fulfilment of the promise of a son by having Abraham sleep with Hagar, Sarah's maidservant. Instead we must continue to rely on God to bring the word about. This, of course, requires patience and obedience as we wait for the outworking of the prophetic word.

9. **Do not substitute the prophetic word for your own walk with God.** In SOL we encourage people not to depend on the prophetic ministry as a substitute for their own personal walk with the Lord. It is important that people rely primarily on the Bible and on hearing God for themselves. The revelatory word compliments and does not compete with the word of God. As always, we place our faith in the God of the word. We focus not on the prophetic promise, but on the God who has promised it. When our faith is misplaced, it produces fantasy and unreal expectations.

10. **Realise the cost.** What God counts as significant will often have great opposition from the enemy. Paul was warned repeatedly about how much he would suffer for Christ's sake.

12. **Timing.** When God speaks to us, we need to allow time for his word to take shape in us. Most words are "invitations" to an end which will involve journeying with God while he shapes us in the person we need to be in order to live in his promise. It is worth the journey. Great benefits will come as we cultivate the character we need to carry God's gifts (see

Ephesians 4:1; 1 Timothy 2:2).

The account of Elisha and the Shunammite woman in 2 Kings 4:1-37 and 8:1-6 is a good example of how we are to steward the prophetic word and to ponder and reflect upon what God has said, even if our present circumstances don't match up to the word.

Notably, this lady welcomes the prophetic by intentionally preparing a room for Elisha to stay when he is passing by (2 Kings 4:8-10), which results in a reward as Elisha says "You have gone to all this trouble for us. Now what can be done for you? (v13) The Shunammite woman receives the promise of a son, against all natural odds, who is born in verse 17 (and later brought back to life by Elisha's prayers). In addition, there is the original offer of a royal reward from Elisha in verse 13 where he says, "Can we speak on your behalf to the king?"

We see a promise that is incomplete and will be fulfilled at some point in the future, but it is not year clear how or why. Some time later in the life of the Shunammite lady (2 Kings 8:1-6) we see her return to her homeland following seven years self-exile from the famine that was prophesised by Elisha. She begs the king for her house and land to be returned to her. God's timing is perfect as Gehazi, Elisha's servant, is speaking to the king at that very moment, relaying the story of this woman and her son, his amazing birth and how he was later raised from the dead.

Because of this amazing timing the lady was able to gain the king's attention and he decreed, "Give back everything that belonged to her, including all the income from her land from the day she left the country until now" (v6). What was offered at the beginning, many years before (2 Kings 4:13) was needed and received much later.

Timing, waiting and pondering are key issues in responding to prophecy and another reason why it is important to record and remind oneself of the prophetic word. We can "receive" the promise even though it may take a number of years to come to fulfilment. Remember, Joseph was waiting in prison before walking out his promise of being a ruler in Egypt where people would bow down to him.

Here are two examples of timing/waiting from SOL members:

"I was prompted to ditch my teaching notes and speak spontaneously and prophetically on Deuteronomy 7:22 for the only time in my life. I wondered why I was prompted by God to do this, until a lady came up to me at the end and said that night was a fulfilment of a prophetic word she had been given with that very verse 25 years ago when she had given her life to Jesus. What is more, she had never heard any sermon on that verse for 25 years until this night, and she almost didn't come to the evening meeting but felt strongly prompted by the Holy Spirit to turn up."

"I was dropping my son at a church meeting with a view to heading home to rest after a long day. Someone came out and spoke to me, inviting me inside to lie down and soak in God's presence and listen to the worship. I felt God say 'Listen to her, she's saying the right thing.' I went inside and rested on a large pink bean bag at the back of the room, soaking in the worship. During this time God told me that, the coming Friday (the next SOL meeting) a man would come in and lie on this very bean bag in this very spot and he would be suffering with a broken heart and would give his life to Jesus. I felt prompted by the Lord to write this down on a piece of paper and to put it under the floorboards by the radiator. It seemed a little unusual, but I obeyed and did it.

When Friday evening came, I mentioned it to just one of the SOL council of reference for accountability and also asked them to keep an eye out for the man arriving. Eventually a man (a stranger to SOL) arrived and laid down on the pink bean bag. During the worship I went over and spoke with him and discovered he didn't know Jesus. He shared he had some big issues and difficulties going on in his life and, currently, he didn't have access to his children which was breaking his heart (the words the Lord had given me). I told the man about the story I had written it on a piece of paper a few days earlier and retrieved the piece of paper. This certainly got his attention! After talking and praying further, the man responded to the love of God and gave his life to Jesus."

4

Living A Prophetic Lifestyle

In the previous chapter we looked at the practicalities of giving and receiving prophetic words. In this chapter we will look at the practicalities of living a prophetic lifestyle. In other words, what should we do in order to position ourselves to be constantly receiving the flow of God's life in us? – to be continually in tune with his voice and acting upon his instructions? I would like to suggest that two disciplines are essential: firstly, the practice of soaking and, secondly, walking in simple obedience. We'll explore both in this chapter.

Soaking in God's loving presence

Talk to anyone and they will tell you that the best way to get to know someone, so that we really "tune in" to them, is simply to spend time in their presence. How much more so with God? We tune into him when we spend time resting and soaking in his presence. As Heidi Baker puts it, we "sow our presence into his presence".

Time in God's presence reveals his character and our identity, as this quote from the Catch the Fire network affirms: "Experiencing God as our true Father, just like Jesus did, will change our lives. Every child of God needs to feel, know, and experience the unconditional, extravagant love of Father God (John 14:6-13; Luke 15:11-32; Romans 8:35-38)."

One of my favourite activities, because I need it so much, is to soak in the presence of my heavenly Father, Daddy or Papa God (the best translation of "Abba"). All of us face the daily challenge of finding the balance between "being" (where we simply sit still in God's presence and bathe in his love) and "doing" (where we respond to his love with acts of service).

J. Hudson Taylor, founder of the China Inland Mission, wrote in his 1914 commentary on Song of Songs (Union and Communion), "Let us never forget that what we are is more important than what we do..." and "...she [the Bride] "did not work in order to earn favour, but being assured of favour, gave her love free scope to show itself in service."

Frequently we find it easier to "do" than "be", so we have to be intentional in creating the space in our lives to be. When we do this, we very soon become lovers of his presence!

What is soaking?

One of the best ways of simply being in God's presence is soaking. In the history of previous revivals in the Church this process was termed "tarrying" or "waiting on God". Revival churches would often spend entire meetings just dwelling in God's presence. This lost art had all but died out, but the CTF network put it back on the map and have pursued soaking since the Holy Spirit outpouring of 1994 in Toronto. CTF say,

"Soaking is simply spending time in God's presence, rather than striving. It's about resting in his presence, experiencing him and choosing to be intimate with him."

As Jim Goll writes, "You are loved because of grace, not because of how well you perform or how dynamic your gifting may be. You are not what you do!" Thank you Lord for the freedom that just happened in people as they just read that. I pray for more Lord!

While we base our theology on the Bible, it is our experiences with God that make his truth come alive in our hearts. When we soak we focus solely on him. It helps us to position ourselves in a place where we are more often able to hear his voice and receive his love. CTF have many documented experiences of people's lives being changed by soaking in God's presence. There have been profound heart changes; marriages have been healed; fears dispelled; depression and sickness have left and lives have been transformed.

Many worshippers have written amazing music for soaking, such as Julie True who has an online soaking centre. She writes, "Soaking is a time to quiet the soul, but to be awakened in the Spirit to hear the heart of God in that moment, and to interact with him in a personal way ... [it] is a time of connecting spirit to spirit and heart to heart with the one who loves us like no other and who created us to have relationship with him." During soaking we do not have to strive at all. It is a time to unburden ourselves at the feet of Jesus; to receive whatever he has for us, healing our soul and body; to perceive what he is doing, to focus on him. It's simply allowing God to saturate us with his love.

Be marinated!

There are currently a plethora of cooking programmes on TV. They advise us that the best way to make meat incredibly tender or pump it full of flavour is to marinate it – and the longer we do it, the better the results will be. Spending time in Father's presence we become similarly infused with him.

Remember the story of Esther in the Old Testament. She prepared to meet King Xerxes for the first time by completing twelve months of beauty treatments prescribed for the women, soaking (marinating) for six months with the oil of myrrh and six with perfumes and cosmetics. After this, Esther would have exuded sweet myrrh and perfume – a fantastic spa treatment ahead of its time!

Let's take another example from the kitchen, a humble jar of pickled gherkins. Gherkins are a variety of small cucumber particularly suited to pickling. The longer they spend in the pickling liquid, the more they smell and taste of whatever the pickling liquid is infused with.

Soaking in God's presence is like marinating or being pickled in God's love! The Bible says that "we are to God the pleasing aroma of Christ among those who are being saved and those who are perishing" (2 Corinthians 2:15). When we soak in his presence, we are infused with his love, grace and mercy, rather than bitterness, shame or anger. Soaking helps turn the *bitter* into something *better*.

It's all about his presence

The presence of God is where we belong. The Father's presence is ours by right. We're not renting it, we don't have to pay a mortgage on it – Jesus has paid for it in full and the legal documents are signed in his blood.

It is the place of true intimacy where we discover our identity. It is the place of love and healing – where we are put back together. It is the place of freedom where our mind is renewed. It is the place where we become aware of the love songs that the Father sings over us (Zephaniah 3:17) as we realise we are loved unconditionally.

It is a place to get rid of our heavy bags; a place of rest for the weary and the heavy laden. It is a safe place from our enemies and the demands of others, where we can pour out our heart to God and be washed in his love.

Of course, God does not force us into his presence. As always, we have a choice. Let's choose to abide in him and be connected to the source of life (John 15:17). Water taps are no good if they are not plumbed into the source and it is the same for us. When we are connected to Jesus, his living water can flow through us (John 7:38). Jeremiah 17:7-8 paints a vivid picture of this:

"But blessed is the one who trusts in the Lord,
whose confidence is in him.
They will be like a tree planted by the water
that sends out its roots by the stream.
It does not fear when heat comes;
its leaves are always green.
It has no worries in a year of drought
and never fails to bear fruit."

This passage teaches us that by staying connected to him we cannot help but be fruitful. This principle is confirmed in many other places, such as John 15 where Jesus teaches his disciples about abiding in him and many of the Psalms. Psalm 84:5-7 says that as we remain connected to God we "irrigate" the places where we set our feet as we carry his presence:

"As they pass through the Valley of Baka, they make it a place of springs" (v6)

When we are infused with Christ we are positive atmosphere changers!

The practicalities of how to start soaking

There is so much evidence and encouragement in Scripture for time spent just soaking in God's presence, but practically how do we do it? Here are some simple guidelines that will get you started.

• The aim of soaking is to get into a quiet place before the Lord, where we gradually shut out the attendant "noise" of life and focus solely on him. It is important then to find a room/location where you can be comfortable and are unlikely to be disturbed.

• Often I start by focusing on one piece of scripture and then spend much of the soaking time listening to a soaking CD (there are many excellent soaking worship albums available, both instrumental and vocal). Soaking music takes us outside the boundaries of traditional worship music. It helps create an atmosphere of total rest where we can receive from the Father and hear him to speak to us. The music you choose will be governed by your personal preferences, but I highly recommend anything by Kimberly and Alberto Rivera or Julie True. Whatever helps you to focus on the Lord and receive his love is right for you. Starting with a piece of scripture before soaking can provide a solid "diving board" to jump off into the pool of God's love. You might find it useful to finish the soaking session in complete silence.

• Depending on the time of day and how awake you feel, you may want to lie down on the floor with a pillow or beanbag under your head or sit it your favourite chair. At this point I want to say that it's okay if you find yourself briefly dozing during your soaking times! We've all done it and it does say in the Bible that while we sleep our heart is awake (song of Solomon 5:2)!

• Turn your phone off and let the answer machine take any messages.

• During your soaking time, the enemy, Satan, the thief who

wants to kill (your dreams), steal (your health) and destroy (your relationships – John 10:10) will try to remind you of all those things you need to do. One way of dealing with this is to keep a notebook and pen beside you to jot down those things and then immediately return your focus to Jesus and carry on soaking. I find that the distracter very soon gives up when I refuse to be distracted.

• A notebook by your side is also useful for recording what the Lord says to you, either through Scripture, pictures or impressions. Mark Virkler, in his series on hearing God's voice (see Ch10's list of resources) makes some helpful points. As a starting point you could ask the Lord what he thinks of you, what he wants to say to you or what he would like you to do. Record what God says to you.

• For how long and how frequently should we soak? It is important to start with a realistic plan, otherwise we will tend to feel we have failed all the time. The time depends on your circumstances, but 10-15 minutes is a good starting point. It's all about developing a habit of spending time with God. Some will be able to jump in straight away; others may find it takes a while to learn how to "be". What is guaranteed is that as you become accustomed to soaking, the time with the lover of your soul will pass very quickly. A half hour soak will feel like 5-10 minutes and you will wish you could spend all day soaking because you feel so restored. As Ecclesiastes 8:3 says, "Do not be in a hurry to leave the king's presence."

This also goes for those times when we might be lying on the floor following powerful prayer ministry. Why get up until God has finished ministering to and restoring us? This doesn't mean that we can't "power soak" i.e. grab any opportunity to soak in God's presence no matter how short. With this mind set we can make the most of those spare moments in life, such as when we are waiting to pick up the kids or loved ones and they are late or we are sitting in a traffic jam. Let's choose life at every opportunity.

• Each soaking time is likely to be different as God floods us with his unconditional love, joy, strength, peace, healing and guidance. As Mark Virkler says, "Prayer comes alive when God does most of the talking" (Ecclesiastes 5:1-2).

• Finally, remember that the Lord enjoys our company. The Lord really delights in you, his Hephzibah (Isaiah 62:4).

I soak on my own, but also at times with others, as I lead a lunch time soaking group called "Pit stop" (which, as the name suggests, caters for people in the middle of their work day who need a few running repairs and fine tuning as a result of the working week). When you get together with others like this it is important to get into the process of soaking as quickly as possible, using a scripture as the spring board, otherwise we all have the tendency to "unpack our agendas" to everyone. It's amazing how, by the end of our soaking time, the things that were so important, making us so frustrated, have been completely resolved by marinating in the love of God. We also ask people to share any scripture, revelation or picture they have received from God during the soaking time which may strengthen, encourage or comfort someone in the group.

The benefits of his presence

I have already mentioned numerous benefits of soaking – identity, acceptance, healing, wholeness, freedom and more. Some will counter that all this sounds very "me" centred; what about the battles that need to be fought and victories that need to be won?

Empowered by rest

I would respond by saying that it is vital our battles are fought out of the place of his presence. It's a bit like the question raised by Martha when Mary was simply sitting at the feet of Jesus (Luke 10:38-42). Jesus said, "Mary has chosen what is better" (v42). Look also at other biblical examples, such as David's mighty men. We read of there being two levels of mighty men – the three and the thirty. The group of thirty were awesome warriors, but the deeds of the three were legendary. The hero of all, the chief of the three, was Josheb-Basshebeth – a warrior who killed 800 enemies in one encounter armed only with his spear (2 Samuel 23:8). Josheb-Basshebeth's name remarkably means "dwelling in rest"!

It is as we rest in God and receive his peace that we see the victories. When all of Israel was about to run like headless chickens as the Egyptians were descending upon them, the Lord said to Moses,

"The Lord will fight for you; you need only to be still." (Exodus 14:14).

Empowered for ministry

Heidi Baker, who has planted thousands of churches in Mozambique, seen many people raised from the dead, seen blind eyes and deaf ears opened and food multiplied (see her book Learning To Love) attributes this dramatic fruitfulness to daily soaking for hours at a time. She contends that the busier she is, the more she soaks to cope with the demands of the day. Heidi reveals that it is out of her intimacy with Jesus that the fruitfulness flows. In her recent book, Birthing the Miraculous, she sums this up by saying "There is always room for more intimacy, more of his presence and more of his glory."

There is no point trying to produce fruit on our own as we can't do it. It's all about remaining in Jesus and staying connected to him. "Neither can you bear fruit unless you remain in me," Jesus says in John 15:4.

Carol Arnott writes in Spread the Fire magazine, "We need to be constantly filled because it is impossible to give away what you have not received." She goes on to relate how soaking has given her a new boldness in ministry. Everyone who has spent time soaking will agree that as our own tanks become full of his love, we can more effectively help the hurt, broken and lost as we overflow with God's love. What is more, the economy of heaven takes over. We find that post-soaking we can accomplish more in one hour than we used to do in a whole day! Decisions become easy as our minds are renewed and have clarity. The perfect antidote for procrastination is to soak!

Hudson Taylor stressed that, "If we are watchful over the souls of others and neglect our own ... we shall often be disappointed with our powerlessness to help our brethren." The signs and wonders accompanying his ministry are well documented and he attributes this to time spent soaking in God's presence. Taylor put it poetically, writing,

"In the secret of His presence
How my soul delights to hide!
Oh, how precious are the lessons
Which I learnt at Jesus' side!
Earthly cares can never vex me,
Neither trials lay me low;
For when Satan comes to vex me,
To the secret place I go!"

Freedom from rejection

The prophetic ministry can only function out of the place of God's presence, as a result of our connectedness to Jesus. There is a certain amount of risk inherent in stepping out to deliver prophetic words, and rejection can be an issue. Rick Joyner writes that rather than focusing on potential rejection, prophets should "set their heart on God's affection and acceptance". Soaking provides an easy environment in which this can happen. Joyner continues, "Dwelling on past rejections will keep us self-centred rather than Christ-centred, which will obviously cause a distortion in our vision."

Rejection, if not dealt with, then invites the next thing into our lives e.g. bitterness (Hebrews 12:15), which in turn distorts our interpretative skills and causes a gradual slide as we find ourselves less sharp, less effective and more rebellious to godly authority. How we respond to rejection is therefore very important. Remember the story in Exodus 15 where the children of Israel arrive at the place called Marah and find the water to be bitter tasting. They began to grumble once again at Moses and in verse 25 we read that,

"Moses cried out to the Lord, and the Lord showed him a piece of wood. He threw it into the water, and the water became fit to drink."

The piece of wood was a foreshadowing of the cross of Christ, thousands of years later, where Jesus would die to redeem us for all eternity and ultimately deal with our rejection.

Filled with joy
Finally, one of the immeasurable benefits of soaking in the Father's presence is simply joy. Joy is the fruit of his presence as Galatians 5:22 and numerous other scriptures attest.

"You have made known to me the paths of life; you will fill me with joy in your presence." (Acts 2:28)

"You have made known to me the path of life; you will fill me with joy in your presence, with eternal pleasures at your right hand." (Psalm 16:11)

"A joyful heart is good medicine, but a broken spirit dries up the bones." (Proverbs 17:22)

"With joy you will draw water from the wells of salvation." (Isaiah 12:3)

Healing and wholeness

A SOL member recounts the following from a lunchtime pit stop meeting:

"One particular day, an older lady and her daughter who were looking around the church for a potential wedding venue accepted a spontaneous invitation to the soaking session following a word of knowledge I had about back pain. We discovered the daughter had a long history of a chronic back condition. During the soaking session, the younger lady received prayer for her back pain and she was instantly healed. On witnessing this, her mother wanted to sit in the chair and receive prayer. She was healed of ear pain and head pain. She also suffered with arthritis and her fingers in particular had been permanently bent for several years. She watched as God released and straightened her fingers. We asked the ladies, since they had experienced the touch of God on the outside, if they would they like to receive God on the inside. Both women gave their lives to Jesus."

Wow! What more can be said? What better place in this book to take time out and go to the secret place right now. In the words of the Beloved Bride to the Bridegroom: "Take me away with you – let us hurry!" (Song of Songs 1:4). Why delay? Go and soak now!

Learning the freedom of simple obedience

The second great key to living a prophetic lifestyle is that of simple obedience. What do I mean by this? On our journey to becoming a speaker of life we speak out only what God says to us and no more. This is so closely linked to soaking in God's presence, where we learn we don't have to perform to be accepted by him, we can simply "be". In the same way, there is a temptation to "perform" with the prophetic gift in order to meet the expectations of others, but we must learn to be secure in our identity in Christ. Jesus learnt the power of doing only what he saw his Father doing (John 5:19) and saying only what he heard his Father saying (John 8:28).

Speaking when he speaks

Kris Vallotton writes, "When God stops speaking, we should too!" Sometimes, when we have a desire to bless someone prophetically, or we are aware of a person's need to receive, it is tempting to try to give a word. But if there is no revelation from the Father, we should remain silent. Don't be afraid to say, "I have nothing right now." Resist the need to say something just to please. We can still pray. We can still be kind and comforting. But we should avoid attaching the prophetic "tag" to anything that is not genuine heavenly revelation.

Mike Bickle refers to this as the "pressure of silence". In an awkward moment we are tempted to give a word we don't have. A test of our maturity and character, therefore, is to refrain from acting/speaking in response to the expectations of others, when we know we have not heard from God. Giving a made up word to someone will not bear fruit and won't ultimately do them any good.

I witnessed an excellent example of this in Toronto a few summers ago. A very well known prophet with an international reputation was the visiting speaker. Many people had travelled to see him (we had journeyed several hours ourselves that morning). He had previously given some amazing prophetic words with great accuracy to the CTF network. At the point in the service when it was deemed time for him to give a prophetic word for the church, however, he stood and waited before eventually saying he had nothing to give. In his own humorous way he explained that he wasn't just going to make something up. Some in attendance may have been disappointed by this, but most were full of admiration. He had clearly pointed to the fact that it was, in fact, all about Jesus and not about him.

Embracing simplicity

Kris Vallotton highlights the fact that sometimes we try to continue speaking when God has stopped because what he has given us seems too simple. "Is that it?" we query. "It can't be that simple, can it?" Kris says, "We don't have to be profound to be powerful."

During a prophetic meeting, one SOL member had a simple picture of the letters C and K written in a very flamboyant way, and the words "be free". Though they waited to receive more from God, nothing else was forthcoming, so they spoke it out. The recipient, a lady, immediately knew the interpretation and application. At school she had always been told off by one particular teacher, just because she always tended to write the letters "C" and "K" quite flamboyantly. The result was that it had seriously subdued her naturally exuberant personality. An ensuing time of ministry resulted in great freedom for her as she stepped into her God-given personality with new confidence as a beloved daughter of God.

Allowing for divine interruptions

Through simple obedience we also learn to do what the Holy Spirit prompts us to do, when he tells us to do it — even though it may interrupt our plans or agenda. A SOL member describes their experience as a visiting preacher for the first time at another church. Keen to make a good impression they had carefully prepared their sermon.

"I was in the middle of the sermon when God strongly prompted me

to stop and ask if anyone had a painful right arm when they lifted it up above their head. I had a choice: carry on with my own agenda or obey (knowing that this was not the usual pattern of things in this particular church's Sunday morning service). Thankfully, I obeyed and sure enough there was a gentleman with that very complaint. I asked him to stand and without going over to him commanded the pain to go in Jesus' name and he was instantly healed. This raised expectations in the congregation and many came forward to receive healing."

Taking a risk, stepping out

If we don't speak out what God is saying to us then no one will benefit. Simple obedience is learning to respond to Holy Spirit "in the moment" and acting on what he gives us. As the Bible tells us, "If you hear my voice do not harden your heart" (Hebrews 3:8 and 15; Psalm 95:8). We always have a choice, so we need to practice obedience. Here is an example from a SOL member:

"I was taking my seat on an USA internal flight and the Lord gave me a prophetic word for the man that was making himself comfortable next to me. Right there and then I had to be intentional and obedient as I was looking forward to the opportunity of catching up on a pressing work deadline. Thankfully, I chose to prefer the agenda of the man sitting next to me. I have seen God work in my life sufficiently to know it was a no-brainer.

I folded away my work and began to converse with the man (who was a top ranking manager in a well known global computing company) and gently brought the prophetic word into the conversation in a natural way i.e. without freaking him out with King James-type speech. We have to trust that the word of God will not return void (Isaiah 55:11) and will pierce the hearts of men

(Acts 2:37). As soon as I mentioned the prophetic word the man immediately became very quiet, drew in a deep breath and then started sharing with me at a very deep level about the hurt of a past relationship (which is what the prophetic word was about).

He commented that apart from his current partner he had never shared so deeply and could not explain why he was doing so now, on a plane with a complete strange! He also wanted to know how I knew. I explained that God loves us so much that he reaches out in different ways to get our attention, so that we will ask him into all aspects of our lives. The man listened and then asked me to write down a prayer he might use to ask Jesus into his life and details of the Alpha course. I wrote down for him the simple ABCD salvation prayer." (see Ch9)

Being obedient when you can't readily see the reason

The victory of Gideon is a great example of when God asks us to take many steps of obedience without our seeing the immediate reason. Similarly, the example of the disciples lowering the nets on the other side of their boat to catch an abundant harvest, even though they had spent all night fishing.

Here are a few stories from the daily lives of SOL members which demonstrate similar obedience:

Salvation in South Shields, UK

"There are times when God says, 'do this' and you do it, without asking too many questions. I was part of a team leading a retreat in South Shields, northern England, when one of those times occurred. In the middle of one of the sessions, I felt God say to me, 'I'd like you to walk out of the church, go up the street and stand on the street corner. Wait there and you'll meet someone and you're to bring them back to the church.' I found myself doing just that and

when I got to the corner I could see no one. I waited for about 4-5 minutes until I saw a man coming towards me. I caught his eye and said hello and told him where I'd come from and what I'd been doing at the church. I invited him to come with me to the church and amazingly he accepted the invitation. When we got there and the person saw what God was doing at the retreat, he gave his life to Jesus. During the weekend, he became integrated with the church and allowed God to work more and more in his life."

Get on the train to begin the journey

"This story has two main scenes to it. The first one begins when God prompted me to get on a train to meet a Christian counselling team. I felt God was going to give me a prophetic word for the leader of that team, but even when boarding the train to start the journey, I had no idea what the word was at all. Knowing that obedience is key, I pressed on with the journey. As I arrived at my destination, God had given me two very specific words. I arrived at the venue and the whole team was assembled, waiting for me and ready to hear the word God had given me. I'd not met the leader before and it was a case of giving the word publicly to the leader in front of their team.

I thought to myself that the prophetic word would either be completely right or completely wrong and therefore it could be the shortest prophetic session I'd ever been involved in. As I gave the word, there was no indication as to whether it was right. It was only later that I discovered the reason for this was because the leader was trying desperately to stay sat on their chair, since both words had been spot on. Both of the words I gave had been given to the leader on previous occasions by well known international prophets, but had not been fully acted upon. Therefore, the leader took this as confirmation that they needed to take heed and act. The leader then allowed me to prophetically minister to their whole team for the next two hours.

What I didn't know was that the leader of the team was well connected to an international inter-government organisation. The connections and subsequent fruit from this act of obedience led me to a plane journey and an audience with a very senior member of this organisation. On the plane journey the Lord gave me a picture of the person I was going to meet showing me that they suffered with right shoulder pain, which had been caused by words of conflict that were spoken over them. Sure enough, on meeting the person in their amazingly long office, high up in the city, they confirmed this was all true. We went through the process of forgiving the people who had spoken the words, blessing them and then we prayed for healing. The long standing shoulder complaint was instantly healed."

Somewhere over the rainbow

"I had been given a prophetic word about a rainbow, linked to the one described in the book of Revelation. In particular, I was due to find the seventh colour of the rainbow which is violet, symbolising royalty and authority. The word also linked strongly with the seven spirits of God from Isaiah 11.

A year later, I was with my family on vacation staying with friends in Muskoka lakes, Ontario, Canada. About 3am, I woke up and asked God about the rainbow prophecy and how it would be worked out. Later that morning at breakfast, one of the friends shared a dream for me that she had at 3am. In it, I had painted finger nails resembling the colours of the rainbow, but the colour purple was missing. Another friend then showed up and shared that she also had a dream during the night and that there was some link between myself and a lady called Gwen Shaw. She then told me that

Gwen Shaw's ancestral home is called 'Rainbow House' in Niagara and to get to it, you have to cross a bridge called Rainbow Bridge. I clearly had a choice as to whether to act on this word or not. A few days and a few hundred miles later, my family and I were walking across Rainbow Bridge at night to visit Rainbow House in order to find the missing rainbow colour. As we were walking across the bridge, I was asking God for confirmation, wondering if it was the right thing to be doing. At that moment, my wife said to me, "Did you see that man who just passed you?" The man was wearing a sweatshirt which said 'Purdue' as in Purdue University. The people who were currently staying in Rainbow House, whom we had arranged to see had the surname 'Purdue'. It was total confirmation. This happened back in 2009 and after spending an hour and a half with the Purdue's, sharing and praying, there has been a significant increase in authority (violet, the missing colour) which has continued to increase in my life."

Guard your heart

There are two final thoughts I want to leave you with regarding living a prophetic lifestyle. The first is the process that the Bible describes as, "guarding our heart, for it is the wellspring of life" (Proverbs 4:23). If we desire to be a channel of God's grace to others, then we need to learn to speak and act wisely. The next verse in Proverbs cautions us to, "Put away perversity from your mouth; keep corrupt talk far from your lips." If we are a speaker of life, then how we speak is very important! An important part of "guarding our heart" is training ourselves not to speak "death" e.g. negative words or gossip. A SOL member writes

"A senior lecturer colleague who had recently become a Christian was having problems guarding his heart, as people kept coming to

his office with choice morsels of gossip (Proverbs 16 and 26 describe the harm that gossip can cause). Prior to his recent conversion he had indulged greatly in this area. My advice was simply to ask God to keep gossip away from his doorway and office. The immediate effect was that people were unable to gossip in his office and would even forget what they had turned up for. It gave him the opportunity to speak life rather than entertain death."

Many phrases have crept into everyday use that, if we think about them, are not particularly life-filled or helpful. We may say, "It'll be the death of me", "It's killing me", "it's just my luck" or "it's been on the cards for a while" (a reference to Tarot reading). The Bible says that the power of life and death are in the tongue. What we speak over ourselves, and over others, can either be a blessing or a curse. I am not suggesting that we get hung up on overanalysing everything we ever say, because God's grace towards us is abundant, but we should be mindful of the words we speak to ourselves/others. Are we speaking life?

Remain expectant

Finally, we should always remain expectant of God moving in and through us. God can speak to anyone, anywhere and in any way. If we are attentive and tuned into his voice, then he can use us to reach out to others and be channels of his love. The following story from a SOL member has two parts to it:

"During a time in his wonderful, loving presence God showed me a prophetic picture of a room in a friend's house, some 300 miles away. We were due to visit them in a couple of weeks. I saw myself and the husband of the house leading a relative of his to Jesus in that particular room. To cut a long story short, during the weekend of

our visit, what I had seen in the prophetic picture actually happened in the very room I had seen in my mind's eye. As the husband of the house and I led him to Jesus, he was delivered very peacefully of many demons that he had given access to his life through many spiritual rituals he had participated in across many countries."

The second part, teaching us to remain expectant for God to move, happened during the week following this event.

"The next week I was at a soaking group in a nearby church, where a female university academic had been invited along for the first time. She really enjoyed the soaking time and being in the presence of God. Afterwards, we were talking and she asked about my weekend, wondering what I had been doing. I felt God say, 'Tell her exactly what happened.' At this point I had a choice, either to obey and tell her the salvation story, or simply to tell her about some irrelevant aspect of my weekend. I obeyed and shared the full salvation story. I then found myself saying to her, 'And you would like to do the same (i.e. give your life to Jesus), wouldn't you?' Immediately, I thought to myself, 'Oh! What have I said?' but the lady responded by saying, 'Yes, that's right.' We spent some time going though what this decision meant and then led her through the salvation prayer. Following giving her life to Jesus, the lady found that doors in her life which had been previously closed for a decade began to open within two months, including obtaining a promotion to professor level in a prestigious university in her home European country (in her own words : 'my dream job'). Yeah Jesus!"

We can be confident that God can and will communicate with us in a flow of life that renews/restores us and flows outward to touch others. Paula Price speaks of the "on going realisation that what you want and need from God already exists in your Kingdom account and all you need to do is withdraw it from the supernatural and embody it in the natural realm". Bill Johnson has majored on this theme (such as in his bestselling book When Heaven Invades Earth) and speaks of the expectancy we should have of bringing heaven down to earth in the here and now.

God doesn't just desire to bless the Church, his people – though he does that, and abundantly – he wants life to flow to all who are spiritually hungry, lost or in need. In SOL we have seen God move in a variety of ways, surprising many with his love and power. Here are some of the ways in which God is working and a few stories accompanying:

- Treasure hunting (covered in detail in the next chapter)
- Business prophecy. This is a prophetic service for business people (of whatever faith or no faith) to provide God's insight to bless their business and in doing so bless the prosperity of the city (Jeremiah 29:7).
- Dream interpretation (covered in Ch7)
- Healing prayer either in the church or outside the church at our "spiritual fayres" or on the streets during treasure hunting.
- Allowing Jesus in us to minister at Psychic fayres. This is something SOL has been involved in for a while. Typically, we set up a stall offering free-Christian ministry right next to other stalls, such as Tarot card readers, Eastern Mystics, Reiki healers etc. Our purpose in being there is to offer visitors a spiritual choice. They can choose the alternative things on offer, or they can choose to come to our stall and have an encounter with Jesus. Here is a small sample of some of the stories:

Back pain healed
"One lady who came to our stall told us she had just spent £80 on

a nearby new age healing stall as she suffered with back pain, but after the session, she still had the pain. We offered to pray with her and explained that we didn't charge. Within a minute, Jesus had completely healed her. She had a lot of questions about who had healed her and our team explained that it was Jesus. Following this, the lady asked if she could receive God into her heart and life."

Healed emotions and shoulder pain

"A lady in her 50s came to our stall and took a seat eating one of the free chocolates that were scattered on the table. God gave me a picture of a 13-year old girl holding a dog. He told me the name of the dog and I watched as it died in her arms, causing deep trauma for the girl. God told me that since that day, the girl had suffered with a fear of tomorrow, rooted deep in her being. I shared this revelation with the lady and she was astonished, confirming that the girl was her and that the story was true and since that day she had felt fearful of the days ahead. Following some further discussion, we prayed for her shoulder pain and it was instantly healed. She then asked if she could invite the God who had just healed her into her life 24/7, 365 days of the year and she did."

Healed knee

"A lady in her 20s came to the stall and she had large amount of swelling around her knee. She sat down for prayer but as we prayed, nothing happened. I felt God say, 'Ask her if she has been unkind to her knee.' I asked her if she had ever shouted or cursed her knee and the lady said yes. She explained that she was very sporty and every time she went cycling, she had shouted at her swollen knee as it kept letting her down and was not as good as her other knee. I invited her to spend the next minute or so saying good, nice things to her knee. The lady really got into it and after three minutes

of blessing we thought that was enough to cancel/break the curse. We repeated our original prayer of healing and we all watched as the swelling disappeared immediately. The team gave the delighted lady some leaflets for the Alpha course at a local church and she went off to meet her partner at the local rugby club to tell everyone about what had happened."

- SOL also provides our own spiritual fayres to the public where we "own" the whole space and provide multiple stalls offering prophetic art, dream interpretation, prophetic insight, music, massage, Sozo ministry and healing prayer. Our leaflets for our own spiritual fayres are designed to be "non-religious" to provide maximum appeal. However, we choose to include the truth of the Bible as a core feature by using the words of 1 Thessalonians 5:23. We call them "spirit, soul and body fayres" i.e. "May God himself, the God of peace, sanctify you through and through. May your whole spirit, soul and body be kept blameless at the coming of our Lord Jesus Christ."

- Working with the city pastors as watchmen/watchwomen for the city (Ezekiel 3:17). Prophets were called "watchmen" in the Bible as they functioned in the spiritual realm in the same way as the watchmen in the natural realm. The natural watchmen were stationed at various points on the city walls which gave them a clear view to watch for enemies and to sound the alarm or to announce the coming of the king or others nobles. The watchmen were trained to be able to distinguish or discern the enemy so as to sound the alarm under real attack. This discernment was important, otherwise on the one hand one could be overly prone to false alarms which would lead to a tendency for people to disregard the alarms or on the other hand being so careless that an enemy could enter the gate undetected. This ministry operates correctly only when it is related to the other ministries in the city. For example, when we see the enemy coming, who do we tell so that it makes a difference? E.g. leaders (remember the watchmen were not the elders at the gate) and intercessors (those who watch and pray, Isaiah 62:6-7). Finally, one important aspect in all of this is to be able to discern what is going on and place it in the context of understanding the times in which the events are taking place, namely the big picture. We are to be like the "sons of Issachar, who understood the times, with knowledge of what Israel should do" (1 Chronicles 12:32).

• Responding to invitations by Christian leaders to pray over cities and churches (to identify unhelpful spiritual activities in particular areas including ley lines).

• Working with other prophetic networks. Our links particularly with Glasgow Prophetic Centre and Light and Life have been invaluable.

• Open doors to speak life and blessing into political arenas, both in the UK and internationally.

5 Treasure Hunting

The Principles

In recent years Treasure Hunting has become increasingly popular as Christians have stepped outside the boundaries of their church walls with a desire to see God move supernaturally on the streets of their communities. What is treasure hunting? It is another way in which we can receive a prophetic word from God and deliver it to the person he wants. People are the "treasure" as we look to discover those whom God desires to bless.

A superficial look over a person's life will usually focus on the "dirt" that covers it, but God is able to see deep within and perceive the "gold" that lies buried under the surface. The heart of the prophetic gift is to "call out" the gold in people. Jesus is our hero and role model in this context. When he met people he saw them with the eyes of God – such as Simon (whose name means "broken reed"), who Jesus renamed Peter (meaning "rock"). Jesus spoke to the treasure he could see in people.

Every person is treasured by God. We are all the apple of his eye

(Zechariah 2:8; Deuteronomy 32:10). Understanding this helps us to look at others differently; to see with the eyes of the Father and call out the gold, the greatness in them. We can look beyond the dirt, the things that irritate, the unlovely aspects, the barriers.

This means that we value people. The ultimate aim of treasure hunting is to let people know that they are valued by God and that he wants to bless them. It is our joy to deliver that message, to bless people, to be good news to them. It is all about letting them know that they are God's treasure and the target of his extravagant love, which he wants to pour out on them. As 1 John 3:1 says, "How great is the love the Father has lavished on us, that we should be called children of God! And that is what we are."

God is always loving and always works redemptive solutions in our lives. It may surprise some to learn that he is always in a good mood – even on a Monday morning when many people are bemoaning the weekend being over. He has a fiery passion to gather in many more sons and daughters of the living God, so he is always about the business of redeeming situations. In treasure hunting, all we are seeking to do is to facilitate God's passion for people. He makes things easy for us in our treasure hunting because he wants people to meet with him. It's important we realise that the moment we step out onto the streets, the pressure is off us and it's all about Jesus. We have succeeded, simply by being obedient to him.

Treasure hunting is not about "arguing" or persuading people into the Kingdom – it's just about demonstrating the good news of the Kingdom. In others words, telling people: YOU ARE GOD'S TREASURE! and allowing God to touch them in whatever way he wants. At the least, it is a practical way of demonstrating to a person how much God loves them. At best, we have seen miraculous healings and more. The person who is healed, right there on the street, will be much more open to hearing about Jesus than the person you are trying to persuade to attend church on Sunday.

Most of us know the issues we have in our lives – the "stuff" that we would like to see changed if possible: broken relationships that we would like restored; pain in our bodies we want to be healed; dead dreams that we would like to see brought back to life. God knows all about these things and his love is able to break through all of them.

A Guide to Treasure Hunting

So how do we start? Here is a practical guide to going treasure hunting on the streets of your community. It is possible to go "solo", but works far better as a team. Gather together some like-minded people and follow the guide below.

1. Distribute treasure hunting sheets and form into groups

The leader of the group should split people into small teams of 3-5 people, depending on the numbers. Every person needs to have a "treasure map" sheet like the one depicted below. This is used to record what they hear from God – clues to the treasure they are seeking.

Ideally, it is better to mix up the teams so that spouses go in different teams, or people from different churches are put together, so that no one knows each other too well. The blessing of SOL is that because there are members from so many different churches, it is quite easy to have groups made up of 2-3 different churches. Why is this important? It helps each person to rely on Jesus and then to rely on each other as a team, valuing each other's different styles/ways of working. It helps us to think outside of the box and not fall into a familiar pattern of doing things.

The Treasure Map

1. Each person writes down the revelation or words of knowledge they receive in the spaces allowed for each category.

A. LOCATION: (e.g. stop sign, bench, digital clock, coffee shop etc)

_____

B. A PERSON'S NAME:

_____

C: A PERSON'S APPEARANCE: (e.g. colour of hair, specific features, colour of clothing etc)

_____

D: WHAT THEY MAY NEED PRAYER FOR: (bad knee, leg, heart, tumour, broken relationships, marriage, emotions etc)

_____

E: THE UNUSUAL: (abstract images such as a lollipop, windmill, lime-green door, dolphins etc)

_____

[SOL adapted our Treasure Map from the more detailed version originated by Kevin Dedmon, which appears in his excellent book *The Ultimate Treasure Hunt*, Destiny Image, 2013]

2. Invite God to speak and record what you hear

After the groups are formed and everyone has a treasure map, we invite God to speak to us and have five minutes of silence where we listen and write down any words we receive from him under the categories on the sheet.

Having specifically invited God to speak, I encourage people to write down what they receive without processing it with their minds too much. Sometimes when God speaks it is like a "butterfly moment" – the word, impression, vision or picture is fleeting; it lands lightly, like a butterfly, and then it's gone again. It's good to capture those immediate impressions and not over-analyse them.

Why do we need to write these things down – why not just remember them? There is one very good reason: when you are on the streets talking to a person and they mention THAT very specific thing God gave you (a particular name, a situation in their life, something unusual), it is much harder to convince them that God spoke to you about it earlier. Better to write it down and allow the person to see it for themselves.

Remember, the exercise of listening to God and writing down what we hear is not an exam – you can leave any of the categories blank. The aim is that across the group you gather together all the pieces of the jigsaw.

Remember to limit yourselves to five minutes of listening and writing (as opposed to spending an hour immersed in prayer, for instance). The reason for this is so that we rely more on the Holy Spirit.

3. Share what God is saying

Once the five minutes is over, the groups can then share with each other what they have on their lists. The easiest way to do this is to take each category in turn and get every person to call out what they have.

This gives everyone encouragement that God is going to speak to people as we head out onto the streets. We do not, at this point, compile a combined list of all the clues. Each person retains their own map as part of the team, but the map becomes the property of the whole team to be shared in a dynamic way, as I will explain.

4. Go out and choose a location

Following a very brief prayer (e.g. less than a minute) we walk out of our meeting place onto the streets and choose a beginning location. If there are several locations listed, it may make geographical sense to go to a certain place first, but if not then ask Holy Spirit to give everyone peace about where to begin. Once at the location, wait and start looking for treasure.

At this point, each member of the team keeps their map accessible, so that other team members can read it. All the clues now belong to the group and it is extremely likely that you will have clues from more than one member that will lead to the treasure.

When we find something on the map, we need to think creatively. For example, leading a treasure hunting in a shopping mall in Toronto, one of our team had the word "Bench", along with the location of "food court" and "smoothie stand". Initially we thought we were looking for a bench to sit on, then someone else in our group saw a person who stopped right in front of us with a large backpack with the "Bench" designer name on it.

5. Speak to people

Once we have identified a person from the clues we've written down, we should approach them in groups of no more than 3 or 4. Larger groups would be intimidating. Bear in mind that a group of mixed age and gender is always less threatening and suspicious. We want to bless people not frighten them!

Choose an appropriate opening line. Something like, "Would you be able to help us? We're on a treasure hunt" will engage people and get them interested.

Show the person the maps containing the clues. In the above example we pointed out the clues "Bench", "food court" and "smoothie stand" to the person to explain why we were talking to them.

We can then ask them to help us by asking if any of the other clues we've written down relate to them. Again, from the above example, the person mentioned that their companion had a headache on the right side of their head – something that had been written on several maps.

People are, of course, acutely aware of their own needs, and once we begin to engage with them, they are often willing to talk about things, such as, "Yes, I'm currently looking for a new job" or "Yes, I have this constant pain that I would like to go." Our clues provide a simple starting point by which we can connect with people and discover more about their needs, which they may request prayer for.

We are always totally open about the fact that we are a group of Christians from different churches who just want to bless people with random acts of kindness – no strings attached. We tell people that they are God's treasure, deeply loved by him, and that he wants to bless them.

Some people do, sadly, have a rather negative view of "religion" (even though religion has nothing to do with Spirit-filled Christianity, though the average person does not make that distinction) – which is why we begin by simply blessing them. We have to be sensitive to people's preconceptions, whilst not ducking the fact that we are passionate followers of Jesus.

6. Ask if they would like prayer

Once we have built a rapport with a person and know something of their needs, we can ask to pray for them, there and then. Most people will say yes, as what harm could it do? Some will be surprised that you then pray for them on the street – expecting you to go away and put their name on a prayer list or something similar. The important thing here is to Keep It Simple.

As Mark Marx says in his Healing On The Streets training, "pray your best prayer, knowing that it is God who heals." Similarly, we pray our best prayer for the person's needs and leave the rest to God. We don't launch into a long, flowery prayer, using terminology that makes us sound like we're from a distant planet in an episode of Dr Who! If, for example, the person has a pain in their leg, pray that the pain will leave in Jesus' name. We can literally say something short and to the point, like, "Leg, be well in Jesus' name." It is easy to understand and gets straight to the point.

Mark Marx teaches that we should always seek the person's permission before laying on hands, and that if we do, we must do so in an age/gender appropriate way.

Remember too we are to value the person we're praying for. If they have a painful ankle and give permission for you to lay hands on them, kneel down and pray for them – even if you have to do so in the rain! Frequently, such acts of servant hood have brought people to tears even before they have been healed.

In SOL we have often seen near-instant answers to prayer as we have gone out onto the streets. Pain leaving hips, heads, backs, ears, fingers, toes, knees etc – usually within 30-60 seconds. We have a significant number of examples of healing which has simply involved holding the hand of the person and commanding the pain in a part of their body to go. We have prayed and comforted people who have suffered broken relationships, who need new jobs, who have exam stress, who are walking through bereavement etc. It is so rewarding to see the look on someone's face when their pain goes or when they feel really comforted and supported by the love of God when they have previously felt so alone, wondering if anyone actually cares for them.

Most people will say YES to prayer. In the event that someone says "no", try rephrasing the question another way, just in case they have misunderstood. But make sure to not trap or corner people, making them feel awkward. Just be ready to bless them and let them go on their way.

7. Let them know where they can find out more

If a person wants to find out more about the loving Father God who has healed them, be ready with a list of recommended churches and details of trusted contact people. Sometimes people will ask who Jesus is and we can give them some "Why Jesus?" Alpha literature, for example. Or they may ask if they can know God for themselves, in which case we can lead them in a simple prayer of commitment.

Remember though, that the focus of the treasure hunting exercise is to bless people and bring good news to them. Of course we want the love of God to become their daily reality, but we are not collecting scalps. Often by demonstrating God's unconditional love we are breaking through the negative experiences or impressions many have of Christianity, so that they will be more open in the future.

8. Allow Holy Spirit to guide you from place to place and person to person

Once we feel that we have discovered the treasure in a particular place, we move onto the next place. If we are unsure where to go next, we can ask Holy Spirit for help. Often we are surprised where "help" comes from. For example,

"On one occasion, our group had clues about two ladies dressed in pink with a bad shoulder and pain in the hip, but we had no location. We asked God for direction and almost immediately a man walked up to us and handed us a flyer for a new coffee shop, saying the words, 'It's in that direction.' We were astonished and explained to the man that he was probably an answer to prayer (which he was quite excited about). We went and found the coffee shop. Opposite it were two young ladies, dressed in pink, who were handing out night club leaflets.

We engaged them in conversation and discovered that they had the pains described on our list (one had a bad shoulder, the other a painful hip). We all joined hands, formed a circle, and commanded the pain to go in the name of Jesus. Both ladies gave surprised, delighted shrieks as their pain immediately went. They wanted to know more about the Jesus who had healed them."

9. Avoid distractions

Keep a look out for opportunities on the way, but beware of distractions. Mobile phones can be a menace in this regard and should be switched off whilst treasure hunting. I give this advice having seen a few gifted treasure hunters sidelined by phone calls lasting 20-30 minutes which ate up most of their time and adversely affected the dynamic of the team.

It is also important to stay united as a team, so it is best not to allow individuals to split off and do their own thing or allow one person to dictate proceedings. Continually ask God to keep your spiritual eyes open and be sensitive as to whether the team should remain in a location or move on. On some treasure hunts, a team may stay at a location for the entire time as it seems to be a hot-bed of clues. At other times the team may move from place to place, having multiple encounters. Each time will be different as the following story illustrates:

"We were in the last 5 minutes of our treasure hunt and had not really had a divine encounter of any note. The few clues we had were "under the flags", "tall concrete pillars" and "a lady with glasses, brown hair and a dark blue top, who has a painful neck/shoulder". Then we spotted some flags on top of the old city theatre, which had ornate concrete pillars. We walked near the flags, but one of our group insisted that we stand under the flags, as the clues stipulated this. This location corresponded to the last pillar. As we stopped and looked to our left, a lady fitting the description of our clues came into view. We spoke to her and she was suffering with really bad neck/shoulder pain. The Lord healed her. She was so happy! This encouraged us to press on to the end so that we could find and bless more treasure."

If you feel you have "missed" a treasure e.g. you notice someone out of the corner of your eye who fits your description, resist the temptation to chase after them or even stalk them. This will undoubtedly make people feel trapped, particularly if you pitch up out of breath and in great numbers! Relax and feel confident enough to let them pass. Our experience is that God will send you many other opportunities of treasures that fit the clues. It makes us hungrier and more alert to spot and approach the next person so that we can bless them.

10. Keep your focus on Jesus

Don't forget this important point. Although most of us will feel a little nervous about the prospect of going up to complete strangers (even though we have good motives and only want to bless the person), remember that Jesus has done this many, many times! What is more, he is the expert living in us. He is our guide and instructor, therefore all the pressure is on him. Let me say it again: ALL THE PRESSURE IS ON HIM! All the healings we will see, the blessings we will see in people's lives, the smiles we will see, the restorations and salvations we will see, the tears we will see and share in, will all be in the hands of Jesus. Do you think he, whose life on earth conquered sin and death and so much more, can cope with the pressure? (do I really need to answer that question?).

How long do we do treasure hunting?

It is good to agree how long a treasure hunting session will last. From experience, an hour is ideal, since it enables groups to remain focused and not get distracted. In addition, people tend to have so much fun doing it, that an hour leaves them hungry to do more and this provides motivation for the next time.

The group(s) meet back at a prearranged point at the agreed time and there is an opportunity for feedback and mutual encouragement/celebration. Depending on the number of groups, it might be appropriate to just share the highlights of each one's experiences. In my experience, all the groups return buzzing with excitement and could provide 20-30 minutes worth of stories, so it's good to manage this process so that each group gets to contribute.

In addition, it's important to steward the amazing stories that people return with; so record the encounters, writing down the names of the people the group met, what was prayed for, the answers to prayer that were forthcoming etc. Pass these on to the leader of the treasure hunt as a record of what God accomplished that day.

In my home town of Newcastle upon Tyne, we work closely with the Healing on the Streets (HOTS) team. We often treasure hunt in the morning and end by making a list of any "unfound" treasure. This is passed on to the HOTS team who are out praying for healing in the afternoon. We have been amazed by how often a person will come and sit on one of the chairs for healing, and something about them (their name, the clothes they are wearing, or their specific need) will fit with the description on a treasure map. The HOTS team show the map to the person and say words to the effect of, "Welcome, we've been expecting you!" This, of course, makes a profound impact on the person, even before they have received any prayer! The cool thing about this is that the person who receives the prayer does not know the persons who had the original clues. In fact, no one on the HOTS team knows either, other than the information was the result of the treasure hunting gang who went out earlier. This way it is so easy for Jesus to get the credit and the glory. I love it!

Treasure hunting stories

There are so many stories that have come out of leading treasure hunting in SOL for four years in Newcastle, in Mansfield (as part of the New Wine School of Prophecy team), Catch the Fire Toronto (Mississauga Campus), as well as hearing from our extended SOL family in the Bethel School of Supernatural Ministry in Redding, California (the home of treasure hunting). Here is a selection which I hope will encourage you:

Suitcase

This is an example of the value of writing words down, even if they don't make sense at the time:

"God gave us three clues for the treasure hunt in Newcastle. The first one was the phrase, 'Always rains, never sun shines' which didn't make sense, but we wrote it down anyway. We also were given an item: 'a black and white polka dot suitcase' and a location: 'railway station'. As soon as we entered the railway station (a good 15 minute walk) we noticed a lady heading into WH Smith who had a suitcase matching the description God had given us. As a rule, we don't follow people into shops, so we prayed that if it was right, God would enable us to have an opportunity to speak with the lady. After a short while, the lady crossed our path and we were able to go and speak with her. We shared with her about treasure hunting and told her that she was God's treasure before showing her the piece of paper with the clues on given to us by God. We waited as she read them. On seeing the phrase 'always rains, never sun shines', she burst into tears. (If we had not written it down she would never have picked up on it).

The lady told us how, only minutes before we saw her, she had been waving goodbye to her husband of 20 years as they had agreed to separate due to his gambling issues, among other things. As she waved him off, she had said that exact phrase to herself and left the platform. The treasure hunting team were able to minister to her, speaking the love of God into her heart and blessing her with his truth. It was an incredibly moving time (we were all in tears). Until this point she had believed nobody cared for her and she was able to leave, knowing God really did love her."

Yellow

"We received three clues from God, namely, 'monument', 'bright yellow' and a series of words including things such as 'clean up the rubbish, remove the dirt' etc. In Newcastle, there is a monument called Grey's Monument, so we headed there to see if we could find

our treasure. On approaching the monument we noticed a crowd of 40-50 Malaysian students had gathered. They were all dressed in bright yellow, holding up yellow banners and signs with slogans such as 'Remove dirty politics' and 'Clean up the corrupt system'. It was a peaceful protest and we headed to the leaders to show them the clues God had given us and to ask if we could pray. The leaders were amazed and allowed us to circulate among the students, ministering physical healing and watching as God set them free from stress and anxiety. It was wonderful."

Dr Fish

"God gave us two clues which didn't connect very easily. The first was 'fish' and the second 'broken relationship'. We thought of a number of places to start looking for our treasure, including fishmongers and the fish pedicure salon in Newcastle called Dr Fish. God used a guy holding an advertising sign in the street to direct us to the fish pedicure salon. As we approached, we saw a man outside dressed as a fish who was advertising the salon. We showed him the clues. He suddenly became very emotional. He shared with us that he had just broken up with his long term girlfriend. He allowed us to pray with him in the middle of the crowded street and we blessed him with the love of Jesus. He was so thankful to us and hugged each of us before we left him and insisted that we take a photo of him and our team, so that he could tell his friends the story that night."

Fruit stall

"Several people in our group had the clues 'fruit stall' and 'bad back'. We were led to pray with two men who sold fruit on a street stall in Newcastle city centre. We discovered that one of them had back pain and he allowed us to pray for him there and then, while he was serving his customers. To his surprise and delight, the pain significantly reduced, almost completely going away. During the following month, we were out on another treasure hunt and walked by the fruit stall. The men recognised us, called us over and the one who we'd prayed for testified that his back was still healed. He gave us a box of strawberries to hand out to people as we continued our treasure hunt. Praise God for his favour."

Bright orange jacket and bone on bone pain healed

'Whilst on holiday in Toronto I was asked by the leaders of the Catch the Fire church campus in Mississauga to model and teach treasure hunting in the Sunday morning service to help motivate people for going out in the shopping malls. Before the service, and before seeing any of the congregation, I completed my own treasure map and put it in my pocket until the end of the service when I read out the clues. There were 20-25 respondees to the clues. One particular example involved the clues 'bright orange jacket', 'black top, black trousers' and 'right hip pain'. The lady who came forward in response to these clues was wearing a black top, black trousers and she was about to leave her house when God strongly prompted her to put on her bright orange jacket before she came to church. She suffered with back pain and bone on bone hip pain which made a grinding noise when she walked. She had unequal leg length, had walked with the aid of a stick for years, and could not bear any weight on her bad hip. Whilst praying with her, God released her hip which resolved the difference in leg length and she was free from the bone on bone grinding. She was able to walk without her stick, weight-bear on the hip, and she continued to be pain free weeks later. How glad she was that she put on her bright orange jacket that morning in response to God's prompting!"

Bleeding condition healed and Bambi

"During the same treasure hunting session in the CTF Mississauga church another lady came forward in response to the clue: "a green top with white patterns". She was accompanied by her husband and she told me that for the past three months she had suffered with continual menstrual bleeding. This was even more distressing than it might ordinarily have been, as the couple wanted to start a family. I invited some women from the team to come alongside to pray for the lady. About 20 minutes or so after receiving prayer, she came back and told me that the bleeding had completely stopped! The following week, she was still healed and testified to the whole church about her healing.

At the same meeting a young boy came forward in response to two of the words of knowledge, 'Bambi' and 'arm pain'. He shared that his favourite film was Bambi and he had some pain in his wrist. I prayed with him and God immediately healed his arm."

It's never too late

When we have officially "finished" treasure hunting it's amazing how often we bump into some previously unfound treasure, so it's often worth keeping our eyes open. Here's a story from a team in Durham, UK:

"Our clue was 'someone will ask for the time'. One student finished the treasure hunt after drawing a blank and was just walking back to college. She was asked for the time by an overseas student. She offered to pray for his one deaf ear. He was totally healed. Hallelujah!"

Eye and salvation

"One of our group had the impression of a "cloudy right eye" and

sensed that as they went out into the city centre they would meet a man who was partially sighted in one eye. Indeed, they did find him and he gave his life to the Lord there and then. Furthermore, he decided not to carry through his earlier plan for the evening, which was to commit suicide by jumping off the Tyne Bridge."

Kosovo

"We had our first treasure hunt this year in Kosovo. What a step of faith that was for the missionaries and Kosovar believers who participated. It was fun and a cultural learning curve, as Kosovars have no frame of reference at all as to treasure hunting in general."

We can all hear God's voice

"A pastor from a conservative church in the USA told me that he struggles to hear God's voice. So, to activate what he had learned about hearing God's voice, we went on a treasure hunt. During the three minute 'listening to God' time the pastor heard the word 'suspenders' (i.e. braces, those straps which hold trousers up!). This was in the middle of summer in Southern California, and the temperature was well over 100 degrees Fahrenheit. The pastor was scared to go treasure hunting and convinced that no one in their right mind would be wearing trousers with braces on such a hot day – surely everyone was in shorts. We went out, but did not find too many clues, and the pastor was ready to give up after 20 minutes. Then, some yards away a car pulled up next to a 'park bench' (another clue someone else had) near a 'green sign' (another clue) and out came 'a lady with a dog' (another clue) and then her husband who was wearing a back support with 'suspenders'!

A few of us began to engage and pray for the couple. The pastor, from a distance, spotted the suspenders and hollered out with his finger pointed straight at the man, 'Hey, suspenders! I NEED TO

PRAY FOR YOU!' The pastor came running up and the lady, who knew this had all been set up by God, was already crying. Her husband laughed and said, 'Well, why don't we all join hands and pray together then.' We did and the pastor prayed for healing for the man's back. That couple walked away in tears, totally blessed and encouraged by God. The pastor was so excited that he had found the treasure that he shared the story with his congregation the next morning. His faith level rose to amazing heights because he had 'heard the voice of God'. It was so cool!"

Jesus is the expert

This story highlights the fact that it is Jesus in us who is the expert. I always say to newcomers, if this is your first time don't worry as Jesus in us has done this a million upon million times and he is very good at his job. In March 2014 we went out treasure hunting with quite a number of people who were coming onto the streets for the first time. In one group I placed two newcomers with an experienced treasure hunter. Here is one story from the hour they were on the city streets:

"We had the clues 'clock', 'time', 'green handbag', 'area of pavement which is bobbled to highlight a junction for the partially sighted' and 'pain in the knee'. We met a lady at the convergence of all these clues with a green handbag. We prayed for her arthritic knee which began to immediately feel better and she was so deeply impacted by the love of God – the fact that she was God's treasure – that she gave her life to Jesus."

Note that this story comes from a group that featured two novices in a group of three.

We should be expectant. Even if you are treasure hunting for the first time, as Jesus is very experienced and knows exactly what he is doing, the pressure is off!

Notable men of the city

"We began our treasure hunt outside the Superdrug store in Newcastle, as it had been our location clue on our treasure map. In addition, we had the names 'Thomas' and 'Harry', 'a bad knee', 'false grass', and 'small bumps'. As we looked around we spotted a fruit and vegetable stall with the food items displayed upon plastic grass which matched our clue. As we walked across to the stall, we noticed that it was situated next to paving slabs with small bumps on them, matching another clue. As we bought some cherries, we talked with the men serving at the stall and one of them suffered with a bad knee and was due to go into hospital for his third operation to fix it. We asked if we could pray with him and he agreed. As we prayed and blessed him, speaking healing into his knee, he felt immediate relief from the pain as it rapidly left his body. He was very pleased and excited, especially as we showed him the clues. We asked him about the names Thomas and Harry, to which he replied in his broad Geordie accent, 'Ah man, do I have to help you with everything?' He pointed directly upwards to a building. The building carried four name plaques of the notable men from the history of Newcastle, including both Thomas (Bewick) and Harry (Hotspur). Two weeks later, we saw the man at his stall again and he told us that he didn't need to have his operation because his knee was fine."

6

Dreams, Visions and Biblical Dream Interpretation

Throughout history God has frequently spoken to his people through dreams and visions and there are numerous biblical examples. Numbers 12:6 records God saying, "When there is a prophet among you, I, the LORD, reveal myself to them in visions, I speak to them in dreams." Then in the well known passage in Joel, the Lord promises,

"I will pour out my Spirit on all people. Your sons and daughters will prophesy, your old men will dream dreams, your young men will see visions." (Joel 2:28)

Earlier in Scripture Job notes,

"For God does speak—now one way, now another, though no one perceives it. In a dream, in a vision of the night, when deep sleep falls on people..." (Job 33:14-15)

Paula Price states, "Anything God says is prophetic because he spoke it outside of our time to be manifested in our era. This is why prophecy relies much on dreams and visions." In other words, God who exists outside of time can "plug us in" to time whenever he likes. Therefore the dreams and visions he gives us can "translate" us into other situations as he desires. Here is an example of what I mean from a SOL member that happened during the writing of this book:

"A friend of mine living in the USA sent me an email. They wrote, 'I've had a few nights of disrupted sleep recently – I'm not sure why. But a couple of nights ago I awoke from a dream, unable to remember any details except that you appeared. I woke up almost immediately and felt in my spirit that you had appeared in order to bring a father's reassurance, comfort and peace for something that was troubling me.'

This was amazing because at the time my friend was experiencing this in the USA, I was soaking in the presence of God in the UK and I found myself in the spirit environment of my friend (I assume in their dream). God impressed on me that my purpose for being there was to speak peace, comfort, assurance and rest."

We are to expect God to speak to us through both visions and dreams, but what do they mean and how do they differ from one another? It is not, as one might think, that dreams happen at night while visions occur during the day. Typically dreams are like narratives through which God will reveal direction or some part of his plan to us, whereas visions are more literal and immediate.

Visions

In visions, God projects images onto the "screen" of our minds. A second type of vision is an "open vision" which we see with our natural eyes as though we are in the scene we are viewing.

On a number of occasions SOL members have attended psychic fayres and set up a biblical dream interpretation table to bring the light of Jesus into those places. SOL has also held its own "spiritual fayres". Here is an example of an open vision one member had whilst at one such event:

"A lady came and took a seat at the dream interpretation table. I knew she wasn't a Christian and as she began to share her dream, I saw a video (completely in colour) of the dream appear above her head. I watched it play and the time frame was slightly ahead of the lady telling the story, so I knew exactly what she was going to tell me before she said it. This gave me an opportunity to ask God for the interpretation before she had finished relating her dream. As she finished, I began to interpret the dream, sharing that it was a warning and that she needed to tune into God rather than the demonic. She had been involved in the occult and things were going very wrong in her life. I felt compelled to tell her that she needed to turn her tuning aerial or 'receiving dish' towards God, just like a satellite dish. After words of knowledge and additional prophetic input, and giving her space to receive prayer, she made the decision to tune into God and gave her life to Jesus. She is now a regular member of our church and going on strong with the Lord."

Types of dream in the Bible

The Hebrew words linked to dreams/dreaming are *chalam* (to cause to dream), *chelem* (to dream) and *chalom* (dreamer). In Greek, *onar* is the most common word for the dreams mentioned in the New Testament (received by Mary and Joseph etc.)

In addition, *enupnion* is symbolic of a dream having a startling effect or there being an element of surprise contained in the dream. In other words, there are dreams that startle or shock, grabbing our attention. Jim Goll highlights an example of enupnion in the Book of Acts when Peter quotes Joel 2:28-29: "...and your old men shall dream [*enupnion*] dreams."

There appears to be three main categories of dream in Scripture:

- **A simple message.** In Matthew chapters 1 and 2 Joseph understands the messages concerning Mary and Herod that are communicated to him in dreams. They are self-interpreted.
- **Simple symbolic.** In Genesis chapter 37 Joseph and his brothers all understand the meaning of the dream, even though it is symbolic, featuring the sun, moon and stars. Again these are self-interpreted.
- **Complex symbolic.** Then there are dreams which require interpretative skills. For example, Joseph the dreamer and dream interpreter has to explain the meaning of Pharaoh's dream. The dreams in Daniel chapters 2, 4 and 8 are other examples.

The source of the dream

It is important to learn to discern from what source a dream has come. The majority of the books on biblical dream interpretation agree there are three possible sources: God, natural man or the demonic. Just as wisdom might originate from Holy Spirit, our natural mind or a demonic source, the same is true of dreams.

1. The Holy Spirit. God frequently expresses different aspects of his character through dreams, so we might expect elements such as destiny, edification, exhortation, comfort, correction, direction, instruction, cleansing, warfare or creativity as he reveals his heart to us.

2. Natural man. There is much speculation as to the cause of normal dreaming, whether they originate from chemical/hormonal fluctuations or are derived from our mind, will and emotions. But these dreams are not given by the Holy Spirit.

3. Demonic. Then there are dreams/nightmares that are oppressive and carry the hallmarks of the demonic, such as fear, panic, deception.

We have talked about tuning into God and ensuring that we are focused on hearing his voice. The same is true of dreams. The more that we tune into God, the more likely we are to hear him speak to us through our dreams.

Why does God speak through dreams?

The author of Song of Songs 5:2 records that, "While I slept, my heart was awake." Firstly, we are more receptive to God speaking when we are asleep, since our resistance is lower and there is less opportunity for our mind to get in the way.

Secondly, God likes to speak to us through dreams so that we will ponder what he is saying to us and, in the process, be drawn closer to him. Proverbs 25:2 says,

"It is the glory of God to conceal a matter; to search out a matter is the glory of kings."

In other words, God loves the process. He could just give us the answer there and then, but he knows we will learn more from seeking and enquiring of him. If God gives you a dream, search out its meaning by going to him and asking for help. We become more kingly by doing this.

I love to run and I have now managed to complete several marathons. When training for my first one, I learned a great deal about valuing the process, not simply getting to the goal. By valuing and enjoying the changes, challenges and rewards of training, I discovered that my value, purpose and identity were not dependent on the race and the one day when it occurred. In the same way, God is teaching us to value the journey; to engage with him and not try to take a short cut to our destination.

Often God will use dreams to prepare us for future events. A SOL member writes:

"I had a detailed dream of a room where I was speaking to a large group of people and certain ministry events were happening in particular parts of the room. The room was semi-circular and I saw all the details, except in the middle of the room where the detail was lost. I wrote this all down. Four to six months later I was leading a retreat in Norfolk, UK, and the main room in the retreat centre was exactly how I had seen it – semi-circular. The middle of the room had several pillars which interrupted the flow of the semi-circle (explaining the break in the room in the dream). Needless to say, the ministry events I had previously seen in the dream and more happened that weekend. I'm glad the Lord prepared me in advance."

Receiving and remembering dreams

Here are some pointers that will help us position ourselves so that we remain open to hearing God speak to us through dreams:

1. Rest and peace. Jim Goll says, "rest is the incubation bed of revelation". In other words, if our mind and spirit are at rest, we are more likely to receive. It is important to guard our heart. As Ecclesiastes 4:6 says, "Better one handful with tranquillity than two handfuls with toil and chasing after the wind."

2. Keeping our receiver clean. Many things can hinder our ability to receive, such as anger, worry, addictions and excesses affecting our mind, will and emotions, unforgiveness and bitterness. We need to have a kingdom mind-set, rather than a worldly one. As Romans 12:2 counsels us, "Do not conform to the pattern of this world, but be transformed by the renewing of your mind."

3. Being wise with entertainment. We need to carefully consider what we allow into our mind/eyes/ears, especially just before we go to sleep (Philippians 4:8).

4. Being mindful of/avoiding distractions (these will be different for different people) – those "little foxes that may ruin the vineyard" (Song of Songs 2:15).

5. Applying the blood of Jesus to the "doorposts" of our heart and mind. Remember you have been granted access to divine protection as a son or daughter of the living God. We can and should ask Father God to cleanse and protect our minds.

6. Meditating on the word of God and praying in the Spirit. This will be effective in positioning us in the right place and keeping our receiver clean.

7. Being good stewards of what God gives us. We value what the Lord gives us, even if at first it appears to be only a little. If we do this, then so much more will be added (Zechariah 4:10).

Write it down

As I have advocated throughout this book, we should always write down the revelation we receive from God. We follow the exhortation of Habakkuk 2:2: "Write down the revelation and make it plain on tablets so that a herald may run with it." In 1 Chronicles 28:19 David said, "All this I have in writing as a result of the Lord's hand on me, and he enabled me to understand all the details of the plan."

It is amazing how much people's dream life increases once they begin the discipline of keeping a notebook and pen or smartphone close to their bed to record their dreams.

How many times have you woken having had a vivid dream, only to gradually forget almost all of it during the day? Sleep specialists say that all of us dream at some point in the night during the Rapid Eye Movement (REM) phase, but we quickly forget. So it is important to make it easy for ourselves to record the details of our dreams.

Dream Interpretation

As with all revelation, there is interpretation and application. There are three key strategies when it comes to interpreting dreams.

1. Simplicity. We begin by simplifying the dream to a few (a maximum of three) key points. The idea is to strip it back to its basic components and build on those. Are there any repeated themes in the dream or is this a recurring dream? For example, Joseph dreamt respectively about sheaves of wheat, then the sun, moon and stars. Both dreams had the same meaning regarding Joseph and his family's future destiny. Is there an area of your life that the dream obviously points to?

2. Perspective. Think about your own viewpoint in the dream:

A) Are you an observer?

If so, the dream is not primarily about you, but you may have a role as a watchman/intercessor in the scenario. Is the central character male or female and do you know them? Are they a leader? Is there a strange or familiar feel about the person? If you have a feeling of familiarity then it is probably from the Lord. If you feel strange or uneasy then it is most likely some sort of warning. Does the person provoke peace or anger? A faceless person is often representative of the Holy Spirit or an angel (who avert their faces).

B) Are you participating?

Are you interacting in the dream, but still not the main focus? This may be a call for you to help others directly.

C) Are you the focus? Are people watching you?

In this case the dream is directly about you and you need to identify where you are (as in the dreams of the baker and cupbearer in Genesis 40).

3. Context. Is it night or day in your dream? Do you have a sense of negative or positive feelings? What is your main emotion – e.g. love or fear? This will help you to determine the source of the dream. Dreams full of fear in the setting of night or that occur in black and white often suggest the source of the dream is not from God, or is a warning of evil intent.

Outside of these three main areas, other features that might help in the process of dream interpretation are:
- The main objects, thoughts and emotions that the dream conveyed
- The cultural context in which you live. In other words, culturally some things will be more significant to some people than others.
- The filter of personal interpretation. In other words, some

people love dogs whilst others are fearful of them, so a dog appearing in a dream will mean different things to different people.

These points provide symbolic and contextual understanding, but it is important to realise that the key to understanding dreams is using a combination of symbolic understanding and the ability to hear God's voice. As the scripture says, "...interpretations belong to God..." (Genesis 40:8).

Practice writing down your dreams and then use the above "filters" to write down its interpretation: simplicity, perspective and context. If you apply these principles, the dream interpretation should be quite short – 4-5 sentences. If you get bogged down in examining every minute detail your interpretation will likely be too long, unfocussed and confusing.

Testing and responding to dreams

In the same way that we respond to and test prophetic words, we can similarly test dreams to judge whether or not God is speaking to us:

- Always apply the Revelation, Interpretation and Application principles described in chapter 3.
- Does it strengthen, encourage and comfort?
- Does the dream contradict or confirm the principles of God's written word?
- Does the dream point to Jesus and lead you closer to him?
- Does the dream "ring true" with your spirit and bring a sense of peace?
- Does it bring life and freedom?
- Does the dream lead to good fruit? (Luke 6:43-45)
- Does the dream encourage unity/fellowship or does it produce

alienation, confusion and disorientation?

• Does the dream line up with God's overall plan for your life?

As with all prophetic words, we must take ownership of it, write it down, pray and ask the Lord about it and share it with those we trust or to whom we are accountable (trusted leaders). Wait on God and God through others for further confirmation/ interpretation before acting on the dream. Seek confirmation at all times. When you act on a dream, take just the first few steps towards its fulfillment to test and approve it as God's will (Romans 12:1-2). Allow the peace of God to rule in your heart and mind at all times and follow the way of peace.

Note the time

It is always worth making a note of the time if you are woken from a dream. A SOL member explains,

"I was very vividly experiencing the love of God being poured into my heart in a dream when I woke up and happened to look at the time. It was five past five in the morning or 5:5. I wrote this down. The next day I asked God about the dream and he pointed me to Romans 5:5. I looked it up and it described the experience I'd had the night before: 'God's love has been poured out into our hearts through the Holy Spirit'. Amen."

Most common dreams

Below is a list of frequently occurring dreams/dream symbols. It is not exhaustive, but is compiled from the teaching and observations of Jim Goll, John Paul Jackson and Doug Addison.

• **House** – commonly represents your life or church

- **Transportation** – vehicles relates to our calling. The size of the vehicle may reflect the degree or scope of the ministry. A car reflects a larger ministry/job/calling than a bicycle. Buses often represent churches. Planes can represent organisations (but is it a civilian or military plane?). A convertible car may represent a particular open heaven time with the Lord. Submarines can represent groups of people who are more covert and who can go deep in the Spirit (represented by the water). Cruise boats can represent groups that are fun and so forth. A sail boat represents freedom, blown by Holy Spirit.
- **Flying dreams** – are more common than you might think. They relate to an increase in spiritual capacity or level and the ability in Christ to rise above problems as you soar in the heavenlies, remembering that "God raised us up with Christ and seated us with him in the heavenly realms in Christ Jesus" (Ephesians 2:6).
- **Taking a shower** – represents cleansing.
- **Falling** – fear of losing control.
- **Losing teeth/condition of your teeth** – usually teeth relate to wisdom. If you lose some teeth and are not able to chew, this can connect with not chewing on the word as much as you have previously and indicates the need to apply wisdom to resolve this. Specific teeth such as loose eye-tooth reflects the ability to see prophetically.
- **Snakes/spiders/alligators/sharks** – reflect the occult. Snakes can represent gossip (small snakes) or if someone is talking about you in a bad way (bigger snake). There is a play on words here as snakes have tails and someone is telling tales about you. An alligator is an indication that someone is opening their big mouth about you. Sharks can represent a lack of peace (forever moving, roaming). Spiders are associated directly with the occult and where people or demons are trying to

harm you, weaving webs, trying to trap you etc. One generally kills spiders by stepping on them with your feet, which is the Gospel of peace (Ephesians 6). A SOL member shares a dream about spiders, "...where I saw a couple arrive at my friend's house and they both had rucksacks. On entering the house they opened the rucksacks and spiders came out all over the house. In time, and after sharing this dream, I found out that a couple had visited my friend's house and, apart from the couple becoming uncharacteristically angry and vitriolic that night, the spiritual climate of the home took a distinct turn for the worse."

- **Past relationships** – the meaning will depend on whether the person had a good or bad influence in your life. A bad influence may represent being tempted to go back to old, unhealthy patterns of living that you have left behind. A good influence may represent renewing your former godly passions or indicate a restoration of good things/ times you thought had passed.

- **Nakedness** – Jim Goll's book deals with this type of dream extensively, covering a number of different applications. These range from the need for greater transparency in your life; a spiritual call to greater intimacy; a cleansing from unhelpful mind/motives; to natural body dreams containing the biological and physical desires that affect most people. In this latter respect Goll says it is, "...not necessary always to spiritualise everything. Sometimes there is no spiritual content. Sometimes a dream is just a dream."

- **Being chased** – often reveals the work of the enemy trying to pursue/chase down your purpose and life. However, on the other side it can indicate the passionate pursuit of God in your life, depending on the context/prevailing emotion in your dream. Is there fear present? Then it is likely to be the enemy chasing.

- **Doors, elevators, stairs, windows, buildings, basements** – doors generally reveal that a change is coming; new opportunities to walk into; elevators or stairs represent transition (elevators are a faster transition) usually indicating that you are rising higher into the next stage of your calling. The numbers of floors you go up can reflect the advancement and the actual number of the floor you get off at can also reveal something (see numbers list below). Windows can represent increased vision or insight (depending on their size and whether or not they are clean). The type of building is important. An office building represents work/administration/your function (new office). A high rise building may represent work, status, level of calling; where you are going or where are you at regarding your calling. If the building is a childhood home then it indicates there are things related to your childhood affecting you now or things that your family has been called to do that you will be fulfilling. Rooms of the house are also important. For example, the basement is below the surface where one can see the foundations of something. Your dream may show someone doing something below the surface/hidden relating to the foundations of the whole building (this can be good, such as killing vermin or bad, eroding the foundations). The attic represents the past or memories or gifts which you have accumulated but are not using. If there is dust present then this certainly suggests inactivity, neglect, or atrophy. The living room represents family/community; hallways are places of transition; bedrooms can represent intimacy; bathrooms are cleansing.
- **Clothing and body parts** – a coat may represent protection/insulation from something. Clothing can represent a "mantle" or anointing. Cultural clothing may tell you what part of a nation your dream relates to and may form part of a calling.

Shoes can represent our spiritual walk and also peace. Bare feet can represent vulnerability to pain or peace/humility depending on the context of the dream. Glasses can represent vision. Earrings, necklaces or accessories can represent gifts from God. Ribbons are reminders of something. A leg or arm not working well may mean something in the spirit that is not fully working yet (i.e. undeveloped gifts or gifts not given over to the Lord). The neck can represent direction or stubbornness depending on whether it is stiff or not.

- **Water, river, oceans** – water usually represents the Holy Spirit and aspects of spiritual life. Oceans often represent the mass of humanity. Being immersed in water can refer to being submerged in the river of God (Ezekiel 47). Rivers can also mean moves of God. Being underwater or submerged can represent the deep things of the Spirit.

- **Scripture verses** – the meaning of the scripture can be for you or to pass on to someone else in your daily life.

- **Clocks and watches** – can reveal what time it is in your life. They may indicate a particular scripture e.g. a digital clock read-out such as in the Romans 5:5 example. They may also represent a wake up call.

More dream symbols

Below is a list of other possible symbols and their meaning, and also a list of significant numbers and colours. These are intended as a help, but as always, please be careful to avoid a reliance on such lists as we want to hear God speak to us, not reduce our interpretation to a formula.

When seeking interpretation of symbolic dream language, the first place you should always refer to is in the Bible, as it is full of parables and allegories. Let's keep it simple. If the dream has a symbol that is the same as one found in the Bible, it is highly likely that the meaning is close to its meaning in the Bible.

After looking in Scripture, God will also speak to us in the context of our own experience, our own geography, and our cultural background. Certain things will have a specific meaning to us personally and not to others. For example, we read in Judges 7:9-15 that Gideon sees a barley cake. It meant something specific to him because he had been raised as a thresher of wheat and barley.

Finally, the same symbol may mean something different depending on the application. In Revelation the "Lamb" represents Jesus as the victor/conqueror, whereas in Isaiah it depicts the Messiah as a lamb led to the slaughter.

Remember, interpretation is a bi-product of our intimacy with God. Even with the tools and categories of dream symbols described below, we still need to rely on the Holy Spirit.

Objects/implements

- **Knife** – severing/cutting off. If you are holding the knife then it refers to holding the word of God (a short knife could mean you only have a limited understanding of the word of God).
- **Gun** – are there any bullets or gun powder? This can represent power or a lack of it. A toy gun represents something that looks like a gun but has no power. A water gun may represent imparting aspects of the Holy Spirit to someone.
- **Dart** – represents an attack (e.g. fiery darts of the evil one, Ephesians 6)

Animals

- **Ants** – irritation/unwanted guests (little demonic attacks that can be painful).
- **Mice and rats** – can represent larger demons (than ants)

that feed off the garbage in your life that you have allowed to be there. How do rats get in? It is often something that is left unattended that will attract them. If there is nothing to attract them then they will not come. Attend to the garbage or unattended things in your life.

- **Cockroach** – again, going after little things that are left unattended.
- **Bees** – demonic attack like ants.
- **Bears** – fierce, unexpected attack.
- **Horses** – power. Can be good or bad (horses of the apocalypse). If the horses are pulling a chariot it may be a sign of God accomplishing your destiny.
- **Scorpions** – the occult.
- **Elephants** – wisdom
- **Monkeys** – the undermining taunts of mockers
- **Moths** – the destruction of valuable things
- **Turtles** – peace
- **Eagles** – prophetic
- **Rabbits** – multiplication or destruction (i.e. disrupting a garden)
- **Pigs** – uncleanness, messy situations.
- **Hamsters** – running in circles, getting nowhere

Significant numbers

Numbers and colours can also important. If you can clearly remember a specific number or colour being mentioned, write this down. The following is a list of numbers that have some biblical significance. These are drawn from various sources including Jim Goll and John Paul Jackson. (See the list of resources in Ch10).

1 = God, beginning, source (Genesis 1:1).
2 = Witness, testimony (John 8:17).

3 = Trinity/Godhead (Ezekiel 14:14-18).

4 = God's creative works (Genesis 2:10), also worldwide, universal as in 4 corners of the earth.

5 = Grace, atonement (Genesis 1:20-23; Leviticus 1-5; Matthew 14:17).

6 = Man (was created on the sixth day), beast, Satan (the exaltation of man above God) (Genesis 1:26-31; Numbers 35:15).

7 = Perfection/rest or completion (Genesis 2:2; Joshua 6).

8 = New beginnings (Genesis 17:12; Genesis 7:13, 23).

9 = Judgement/salvation (Matthew 27:45; Galatians 5:22-23).

10= Law (Exodus 34:28; Exodus 20).

11= Incompleteness (Genesis 32:22); also transition between 10 and 12.

12= Apostolic (Revelation 7; Matthew 10:2-5; Leviticus 24:5-6)/ government.

13= Rebellion (Genesis 14:4; 1 Kings 11:6).

24= Priesthood and order (Revelation 4).

50= Liberty, freedom, Pentecost, Jubilee (Leviticus 23, 25; Acts 20:16).

Doubling, tripling and other multiples of these numbers often have the same meaning, but with an increased intensity of the meaning behind the number.

Significant colours

Paula Price writes that the prophetic use of colour is quite natural: "Different colours surround prophetic manifestations to denote the spiritual agents that minister the material fulfilment of God's word."

- **Red:** like most of the colours, the meaning depends on the context e.g. royalty or power. Red can also mean war, peace, anger, bloodshed, sacrifice, atonement (Isaiah 1:18, Revelation 6:4; 12:3; 2 Kings 3:22, Joshua 2:18-21).

- **Orange:** the fire of God, harvest of a season, spirit of wisdom (Isaiah 11:2-3), perseverance.
- **Black:** calamity, sin, death or famine (Lamentations 4:8; Revelation 6:5 and 12; Jeremiah 4:28 and 8:21).
- **Brown:** of the earth, dead (as in plant life).
- **Blue:** Heaven, revelation, Holy Spirit (Numbers 15:38), shalom, communion. Blue was the colour of the cloth used to cover the sacred utensils and implements of service used by the priests (Ezekiel 23:6; Exodus 25:4).
- **Purple:** kingship, authority, royalty (John 19:2; Judges 8:26).
- **White:** purity, light, righteousness, holiness and success, victory (Revelation 6:2; 7:9, 19:14).
- **Gold:** the refining of the Spirit, kingdom glory, wealth.
- **Green:** wealth, prosperity, generosity, growth, life, hope, sowing and reaping, spirit of counsel and prophetic operation (Isaiah 11:2-3).
- **Yellow:** heavenly insight (supernatural illumination), light, joy, celebration, glory revealed.
- **Violet:** inheritance, intimacy as a child of God, rest, the colour of amethyst (violet) is the twelfth foundation stone in the New Jerusalem (Revelation 21:20). In Hebrew, amethyst is associated with dreams, which is why the New age movement has picked up on this aspect.
- **Silver:** redemption, wisdom. Israel's new leaders were each to offer seven silver platters upon inauguration to their offices. In the wilderness the Israelites were required to give half a shekel of silver for their redemption and Jesus was sold for silver in order to redeem us.
- **Indigo:** deliverance, authority in warfare, freedom, hiddenness.

Back to school

Finally, the only way to begin is to interpret some dreams. Practice on other, like-minded people in a safe environment and give each other permission to get it wrong and make mistakes. In my early days I was blessed by people being prompted by God to come up to me spontaneously and ask if I could interpret their dreams. Latterly, I have been blessed by a number of people who have at least 5-6 dreams a night which they record and send to me. Or they tell me their "best" dream and expect an interpretation on the spot! This is all good practice. As always, be open as to the form of the interpretation. Here is an example from a SOL member:

"I was reading the account of Daniel in the Bible about how God allowed him to know King Nebuchadnezzar's dream without the king telling it to anyone. What is more, Daniel interpreted the same dream. I said to the Lord that if he did this for Daniel, I would like to be used in the same way. The following month I was ministering at a church in Canada and I saw an open vision of a video scene played out over a person's head and I received the interpretation of the scene. The astonished recipient said that I had seen a dream that they'd had several years ago and that no one had been able to interpret. Thank you Jesus. I thought to myself, ask and we will receive."

7

Nurturing The Prophetic Part 1:

Growing in the prophetic as an individual

In this chapter we will look at how to nurture the prophetic in our lives as individuals and how we can create a culture of welcoming the prophetic in our churches.

Growing and going deeper

Growing in the prophetic is not an area of our spiritual lives that is isolated from the rest – it should be seen as part and parcel of our growing into an ever-deepening, ever more intimate relationship with Jesus. To that end, we will grow in the prophetic if we simply focus on upgrading our relationship with him, stepping into the next phase of our journey. Let's examine this a bit more.

Being hungry to grow in the prophetic goes hand in hand with our hunger to press into God and walk in our destiny and calling. As Song of Songs 3:4 so beautifully expresses,

"When I found the one my heart loves; I held him and would not let him go."

Heidi Baker writes in her book, Birthing the Miraculous,

"Most of us have had a vision, a calling, or dream from God at one time in our lives. It is likely that not all of what God has shown us has come to pass. If we are to accomplish all He wants for us in this life, we must always desire more of him ... Our passion will continue to live and burn as long as we cultivate a holy hunger, positioning ourselves to be overshadowed again and again, looking deep into the eyes of Jesus ... I pray that you would be drawn to feast upon God's goodness in the secret place and that you would rest in him at such a deep level that yielding to his will becomes easy. May you be one who is not content to go anywhere without his presence."

So what are the common stages in the process of walking into our calling and growing in God? There are several aspects listed below, but first we have to recognise that our walk with God never remains static. He takes us through various times and seasons on our journey. Sometimes we enjoy a season so much that we set up camp there and become reluctant to move on, but we have to recognise when God calls time on a particular season and wants to usher in the next.

Recognising the season

Ecclesiastes 3:1-8 reminds us that there is a season for things and that when one season is finished, then it is time to move on. When we sense God is calling us to move to the next stage, it's important we don't resist him. There are some good reasons why we must move on:

1. The anointing is in the new season

If we refuse to move and keep on doing what we've been doing, we will miss out on all God has for us. God's anointing and blessing for us will be in the new horizons and opportunities he has created for us. In addition, the old ways which we are stuck in are unlikely to remain light and easy to carry. If we carry on with the old when God has moved on, things will become laborious for us, sapped of the joy we once knew.

2. Holding onto the old inhibits the new

In addition, when we refuse to relinquish our current position, it's highly likely that we are inhibiting someone else taking hold of their destiny. Often, especially in ministry, when we move into a new season, God has appointed a replacement for us. Successors are good news because they release us to be able to take our next step.

Isaiah 28:24-29 contains godly wisdom that illustrates the biblical principle of growing, maturing and moving on at the right time:

"When a farmer ploughs for planting, does he plough continually? ... Does he not plant wheat in its place ... grain must be ground to make bread; so one does not go on threshing it forever."

God always prepares the way for our next step (Isaiah 45:2-4). Our steps of destiny will be contested by the devil, but we know that as we take the step prompted by the Lord, he will not let us down. He will keep us, guide our steps and illuminate our path (Psalm 119:105, Song of Solomon 7:1, Ephesians 6:15; 1 Samuel 2:9; 2 Samuel 22:34; Psalm 18:33' Habakkuk 3:19; Psalm 18:36; Psalm 121:3; Isaiah 52:7; Nahum 1:15).

Five steps for going deeper and moving into our calling

Here are some incredible truths to consider as we seek to deepen our relationship with Jesus. The most incredible thing is that God loves us so much that he is pursuing us far more urgently than we are pursuing him! And he wants to release us into a deeper level of incredible, liberating freedom. As Job 36:16 tells us,

"He is wooing you from the jaws of distress to a spacious place free from restriction, to the comfort of your table laden with choice food."

Step 1 – Father God is pursuing intimacy

First, there is the incredible truth that Father God is wooing us. He actively pursues us and calls us to go deeper with him. "Arise, my darling, my beautiful one, come with me," he says in Song of Songs 2:10. He takes such great delight in us that his desire is to bring us to a wonderful, spacious place of calling.

"He brought me out into a spacious place; he rescued me because he delighted in me." (Psalm 18:19)

Step 2 – The Lord is opening a door of hope

We may feel that at present we are experiencing a hard time, a season of distress or trial. We may go through something like this for a season, but we have a sure hope as Father God promises to take us out of the "jaws of distress". His plan is always to transform our present troubles and constriction by opening a door of hope. In Hosea 2:14-15 we see this principle at work:

"Therefore I am now going to allure her … and will make the Valley of Achor a door of hope."

Once again we see God wooing. In Hebrew, achor means "trouble". It was the place where Achan and his family were stoned to death for the sin of plundering the spoils of battle (money and idols) and defiling the camp, bringing trouble upon Israel (see Joshua 7:10-26). Hosea encourages us that no matter what trouble we are experiencing, God will turn it around. The life of Joseph is another example of how God moves us from a place of turmoil and trouble to a place of liberation and blessing. Jesus is our ultimate "door of hope", as John 10:9 says:

"I am the gate [or door]; whoever enters through me will be saved.

They will come in and go out, and find pasture."

Step 3 – he is taking us to a spacious place, free from restriction
God rescues us into a spacious place simply because he delights in us. This promise of a spacious place runs through many scriptures, such as 1 Chronicles 4:9-10 (where we are called to enlarge our territory in the prayer of Jabez), Psalm 31:8, and Isaiah 54:2-3 where we read,

"Enlarge the place of your tent, stretch your tent curtains wide, do not hold back; lengthen your cords, strengthen your stakes. For you will spread out to the right and to the left."

In Genesis 26 we read of Isaac re-digging old wells that Abraham had dug, and which the Philistines had blocked up. He named one well Rehoboth, which means "wide open spaces". Verse 22 reads,

"He named it Rehoboth, saying, 'Now the Lord has given us room and we will flourish in the land.'"

The whole of process of re-digging the wells of revival which our forefathers had dug, but which the enemy has blocked, could fill another whole book!

Step 4 – It requires an act of will
The door of hope from trouble to the spacious place God has prepared is open, but it requires an act of our will to walk through it. We actually have to move! There are two aspects to this.

First, we have to fully let go of what we have now in order to take hold of that which God has for us. We are to reach out for our destiny with both hands. We wouldn't attempt to open a closed door whilst carrying a heavy box. Instead, we would put it down so that we could open the door properly. In the same way, we have to relinquish the heavy things of the past we are carrying to free ourselves up to walk into our future. If we need help to move into our spacious place, God will graciously provide it.

"How I carried you on eagle's wings and brought you to myself." (Exodus 19:4)

For me, this verse always conjures up images of the eagles in Lord of the Rings who transported the Hobbits and their friends out of danger to a place of safety. If we are struggling, we only need to cry out to Father God and he will bear us up like an eagle.

Secondly, we need to commit to reaching our destination. There is no point standing in the doorway of destiny, looking in. We need to walk through it. Let's not be like Abraham's father, Terah, who began journeying well, but only got half way and finished badly (Genesis 11:28-32). Terah and his family left Ur bound for Canaan, the Promised Land, but stopped on the way at Harran and settled there. It was left to his son to complete the move and walk into the fullness of his inheritance and calling (Genesis 12:1-2).

Step 5 – your destiny is unique

Your destination is completely bespoke; tailor-made for you. Song of Songs 2:4 says, "Let him lead me to the banquet hall, and let his banner over me be love." God has a sumptuous feast waiting for you that is infinitely better than any expensive restaurant you could care to imagine. It is a place of God's extravagant goodness, overflowing with the excess of his love towards you. Now that's what I call a destination. As Psalm 36:8 reads:

"They feast on the abundance of your house; you give them drink from your river of delights."

This table is prepared before our enemies as we are anointed with God's overflowing grace and goodness (Psalm 23). Let's not settle for meagre scraps or yesterday's stale rations when it is the Lord's delight to satisfy us with the abundance of his house.

Embrace humility, let go of pride

Letting go of former things really is key in the process of moving forward in our spiritual lives. In this, humility is our greatest asset.

Jonah wrote that, "Those who cling to worthless idols forfeit the grace that could be theirs" (Jonah 2:8).

An idol is any thing that we elevate above Jesus in our lives. When the word "idol" is mentioned we tend to think of statues of false gods, or perhaps an unhealthy attachment to some overarching pursuit that consumes all our time and energy. But often our "idol" is our reliance upon our own initiative and efforts to get the job done – i.e., we attempt to take our destiny into our own hands.

Ecclesiastes wisely says, "Better one handful with tranquillity [the peace of God] than two handfuls with toil and chasing after the wind" (Ecclesiastes 4:6). What are we chasing after, rather than waiting on God for? Who or what are we clinging to or relying upon?

King Uzziah was a man who started well by relying on God and saw many victories as a result. But once he had attained his lofty position, he fell into the trap of self-reliance. He became proud, full of his own self-importance, and finished badly (2 Chronicles 26:16-18). "God opposes the proud but gives grace to the humble" (James 4:6). Humility is the answer to starting well, living well and finishing well, in the flow of God's grace. 1 Peter 5:5 reiterates James' exhortation to "clothe yourselves with humility towards one another, because God opposes the proud but gives grace to the humble."

If humility is the antidote to pride, then how do we define it? I like Kris Vallotton's definition. "True humility is not thinking less of yourself, but thinking of yourself less. The truth of God's grace humbles a man without degrading him and exalts a man without inflating him. Humility is not demeaning yourself, it is exalting our

God." What does this mean in relation to the prophetic?

Let God promote you

Rick Joyner writes that, "humility is a safety net" for the prophetic as "we seek humility before position". He continues to explain that there is a simple factor that distinguishes false prophets from genuine ones:

"False prophets use their gifts for their own ends, in order to build up their own influence or ministry. True prophets use their gift in a self-sacrificing way, for the love of Christ and the sake of his people."

Elsewhere, Rick points out that this is not to conclude that our motives must be absolutely pure before we can be used by God (otherwise none of us would ever be involved in ministry), but it helps us to notice and guard against signs of self-seeking, self-promotion and self-preservation in our ministry.

Having accountable relationships in place is a must for prophetic ministry, because they can provide an early warning system which can lovingly but firmly point out any "self activities" and guide us back to Christ-centred rather than self-centred ministry.

John 7:18 helps us in our spiritual check-up:

"Whoever speaks on their own does so to gain personal glory, but he who seeks the glory of the one who sent him is a man of truth; there is nothing false about him."

Kathryn Schulz wrote an interesting article entitled "The Self in Self-Help" (New York magazine, January 2013). The subtitle to her piece says it all: "We have no idea what a self is. So how can we fix it?" When we focus on being Christ-centred rather than self-centred we position ourselves for God to be able to work with us. The answer to the snares and pitfalls of self-promotion is to allow God to promote us, lifting us up at the right time.

We need to have a high level of confidence that God knows what he is doing in our lives, accepting the wonderful upside down economics of the Kingdom where, "...those who exalt themselves will be humbled, and those who humble themselves will be exalted" (Matthew 23:12). One of Heidi Baker's classic messages is simply called, "How low can you get?" (which was followed up by a similar message called "Lower still"!). Heidi implores us to leave God in charge of any promotion in our lives. A story from a SOL member further highlights the principle:

"About 10 years ago I travelled to the then Toronto Airport Christian Fellowship (now CTF). I had been given a prophetic word for 'someone on the leadership team'. I was unknown to the leaders and thought to myself, 'Who am I? I can't just go up and say I've got a word for the leadership team.' But I trusted that God would somehow make a way. At the end of the Sunday morning service I was approached by Duncan Smith, one of the leaders. Duncan is British and so am I, so we began chatting. After a few minutes he said that God had told him that I had a prophetic word for him, and he invited me to go to his office the next day so that I could share it with him.

The next day I arrived at his office and as soon as I began to share the word, God threw Duncan to the ground where he stayed for more than an hour. It was a really powerful encounter for him. Afterwards, as Duncan was seeing me out, we blessed some of his team. The power of God was so present that one man in particular fell under the Spirit in the team office as we were walking towards, while we were still some distance away. Duncan then invited me to give the same word at an evening meeting that he and John Bootsma were leading that day. The sharing of the same word that evening facilitated the transition into immediate ministry and

I found myself ministering with Duncan to the congregation for the rest of the evening. Duncan subsequently became a great friend. I'm so glad I put my trust in God, rather than trying to make something happen myself."

We can walk forward with complete confidence in Jesus to accomplish our destiny and purpose in life. Even when we feel like we have no "map" for the bespoke territory God is taking us into, we need not worry because Jesus is ever our forerunner. You may have heard this biblical phrase and pondered its meaning. It stems from ancient eastern terminology and was connected to ships entering harbour. If a ship was very large or had problems getting into harbour due to storms, a "forerunner" would be sent ahead. This was a smaller vessel that could navigate the choppy water and literally carry the anchor ahead to a place where it could be firmly lodged and the larger ship winched into harbour. Hebrews 6:19-20 tells us that Jesus is our spiritual forerunner:

"This hope we have as an anchor of the soul, a hope both sure and steadfast and one which enters within the veil, where Jesus has entered as a forerunner for us, having become a high priest forever according to the order of Melchizedek."

This is so encouraging. Jesus is our forerunner. He died on our behalf and went ahead of us into Heaven. Our lives are anchored in him and he will winch us out of trouble and into safe harbour – our destiny which has been proclaimed in Heaven. This should be a game-changer for each one of us, as we realise that we have full permission from God to approach the throne of grace with confidence, boldness and courage (Hebrews 4:16), totally loved by our heavenly Papa.

8

Nurturing The Prophetic Part 2:

Growing corporately in the prophetic

In the previous chapter we looked at the vital issue of positioning ourselves to move forward with God into our destiny and calling. Unless we follow those principles, letting go of the past, vanquishing self-effort, and allowing God to promote us, then we cannot flourish in our gifting. But if we relinquish control of our lives to Jesus, then we can begin to grow our prophetic gift, both individually and corporately.

In this chapter we look at very practical ways in which we can both a) practice the prophetic and b) encourage the growth of prophetic communities. Samuel provides a great biblical example of how to nurture a prophetic community. Writer Kevin Horn pinpoints the fact that Samuel was an "apostolic prophet" – in other words, a "shepherd-prophet". The starting point for training the body of Christ in the prophetic is simply the gathering together of like minded individuals who are hungry to hear God speak. The shepherd-prophet has a role to play in facilitating the gathering and activating the gift.

Practice, practice, practice

At every level there is a continual process of growing our prophetic gifting. Kris Vallotton takes the example of Jesus' parable of the talents, writing, "If we use what we have received, more will be given to us" (Matthew 25;14-28). Spiritual gifts are meant to be used and can become dulled and ineffective if we don't keep them sharp. Instead we need to put them to work (1 Timothy 4:14-15). The Holy Spirit doesn't need any practice at all to do what he does – but we need much practice in improving our ability to flow with him and what he is doing.

Below I have included a list of "prophetic activation exercises" that we use in SOL to nurture and grow the prophetic gift. These can be used as part of regular prophetic training days or incorporated into prophetic gatherings. Feel free to try any of them, whilst remembering that it is important that people are allowed to "test" their gift in a safe environment. A safe environment is one in which the name of Jesus is lifted high, the Holy Spirit is welcomed, we are ministering out of the Father heart of God, following the way of love, and in which people are allowed to make mistakes.

It bears repeating that we must give each other permission to practice, guided by the core purpose of prophecy – to strengthen, comfort and encourage. My experience has been that, although we will make mistakes and some words won't be 100% accurate, the people we prophesy over will be bowled over by the golden nuggets you have spoken that have come from the throne room of Heaven. They tend to focus on the gold and filter out that which is irrelevant or inaccurate. We also find this to be the case when we take prophecy out onto the streets. People so amazed by the revelation that connects with them, that they are prepared to overlook the odd mistake.

We must overcome our propensity to think, "What will happen

if I get it wrong?" As Jim Golls says, "Our goal is not to be known by being right or the best. Our goal is that Jesus Christ may be made known! With proper foundations in place, proper ministry may proceed forth."

So in all the activation exercises below, focus on all the positives, rather than the negatives, that come out of them. A perfectionist mind set will paralyse you, so that you end up doing nothing. Instead, as Bill Johnson has said, pursue excellence rather than perfection. Perfectionism will inhibit and trap us. If we get something 99.9% of something wonderfully and excellently correct, perfectionism will always focus on the 0.01% that was wrong and we'll still feel like a failure. But pursuing excellence will always free us and help us to spread our wings.

Prophetic activation exercises

1. Prophetic triplets. This is a very easy starter exercise. Get into a group of three people, preferably with people you don't know well, avoiding close friends and spouses. Give each person a different number from 1 to 3. The exercise consists of three rounds (one round per person as the recipient) and each round consists of three phases.

Round 1: Person number 1 is the recipient and numbers 2 and 3 are listening to God and delivering the prophetic encouragement.

Phase (a): All goes quiet and numbers 2 and 3 have a few minutes to listen to God. If people have not done this before give them three minutes to listen. For more experienced people one minute is ample. Revelation may come in the form of a vision, scripture, picture etc.

Phase (b): This is an opportunity for numbers 2 and 3 to share with person number 1 what they have received from the Lord. Here I refer back to Revelation, Interpretation and Application (see Ch2). If someone receives revelation but is not sure what it means, they should share it anyway. The other person sharing may have something that compliments what is said or may separately receive the interpretation. What is guaranteed in this phase is that if you do not open your mouth the recipient will never hear what you have to say! In this phase numbers 2 and 3 are doing the talking while number 1 just listens.

Phase (c): This is the feedback phase. Person number 1 can encourage numbers 2 and 3 mentioning words that have resonated with them, which have spoken into their lives and situation. This also provides an opportunity for number 1 to seek clarity on any word that resonated but that they didn't quite understand. This phase usually lasts for 3 minutes.

Rounds 2 and 3 follow on, repeating the phases above, but with each of the other people taking a turn to be the recipient. As always, it is so helpful to write down the revelation that is received, which helps to avoid any confusion in delivering the word and allows the person to take it away and submit it to trusted advisors etc.

It is also helpful for one person to act as timekeeper for all the participating groups, to ensure that all phases start and finish simultaneously, meaning that each group is working on the same phase at the same time. I sometimes use a loud ship's bell to announce the transition of each phase, because I want this to be a fun time of learning and practicing. If this exercise is new to people, it is encouraging to go around the groups at the end asking each group to provide feedback and examples.

2. Prophetic envelopes. This works very well on a training evening or during a day/weekend retreat. At the beginning of the session hand out blank envelopes to everyone and get them to clearly write their name on the front of the envelope in block capitals. These envelopes are placed unsealed on a table which is easily accessible. The idea is that people can place written prophetic words that strengthen, encourage and comfort into the envelope. To ensure that there are several pieces of paper in each envelope by the end of the session, we ask the people sitting either side of an individual to begin the process of populating their envelope. After this, people are free to put a word into any envelope at any time. At the end, the owner of the envelope will take it away and read the contents – but only at the end of the session, in order to reflect and be encouraged.

3. Prophetic circle. In smaller groups (five works well) form a circle. The first person speaks words of life to the person on their right. If the receiving person does not have a recording device (e.g. a smartphone) then the person to the right of the receiving person writes down the words/pictures for them. Allow three or four minutes, so that the receiving person can ask for clarification and provide quick feedback so that all can hear and be encouraged. Continue the pattern until everyone in the circle has been a recipient.

4. Popcorn or speed prophecy. With people arranged either in two lines or two circles (inner and outer) this is a rapid fire prophetic session based around biblical characters, a fruit of the Spirit, or a simple word of destiny. I love this exercise because it is fast moving, dynamic and great fun. First, arrange people in two lines facing each other so that everyone has a partner. If there are a lot of people and space is a challenge, an outer/inner circle may work better. Ensure everyone has a partner. Now choose one of the following exercises:

a) An ice-breaker – the first group of people ask God to bring to mind a character from the Bible who they identify with the person opposite. It may simply be a name like "David" or "Esther", but ask God for a little bit more detail. For example, you might say, "The Lord is with you, might warrior" (e.g. Gideon), or "You have been raised for such a time as this" (Esther). "You are an extravagant worshipper" (David) etc. Allow a minute (or two at the most if people have not done this before) for this to be communicated. Then repeat the process reversing the partnership. Next, move each person on one place, so that they are working with a new partner.

b) A variation upon the above is to choose a fruit of the Spirit (love, joy, peace, goodness, patience, kindness, faithfulness, gentleness, self control) or a word of destiny that you feel God speaking about the person/their calling.

c) Words of life. Once they are comfortable with the mechanics of this, you can repeat the above with people prophetically speaking out words of life over each other in a rapid, dynamic, popcorn popping format. Sometimes, like trying to start a car on a cold morning, people may need a jump start. If so, encourage people to begin speaking out their favourite life giving scripture to get their prophetic engine going and the rest usually flows.

5. Blindfold prophecy exercise. A variation on the prophetic lines/ circles described above is to have the inner circle close their eyes completely, while people in the outer circle walk around, stopping opposite a random person in the inner circle. When everyone is in place, the person in the outer circle will lightly touch the forehead of their their inner circle partner to let them know that there is someone opposite. This is the signal for the inner circle person (who is still keeping their eyes closed), to begin to prophesy words of life to their counterpart – not knowing who that person is. Allow two or three minutes for this part of the exercise. Then the inner circle person opens their eyes and there is a feedback session lasting three minutes. The wonderful thing about this is that the person in the inner circle is learning to rely on the Holy Spirit's prompting, rather than what they see before their eyes.

This exercise may seem a little risky in terms of guaranteed outcomes, but I can assure you that over the years we have done this, it has been well worth it. The encouragement and testimonies have been fantastic. Interestingly some people (including my wife, Juliet) find it easier to have prophetic words using the "blindfold format", simply because in other contexts they tend to argue themselves out of saying something because of what they visually perceive about the person. For example, one SOL member spoke about their counterpart in terms of God speaking to them through precision, physics and complicated intellectual matters. When they opened their eyes, the person opposite was a physics student. This may have been obvious to the speaker, so that they wouldn't mention it.

6. "Blindfold" prophecy on the streets. Here is an example story that shows how at SOL we practice and train so that we can go out on the streets and bless others.

"We were doing a SOL stall at a psychic fayre in a small market town in Northumberland, England. During my lunch break, I was in a café when God told me that the person behind me in the queue (who I

had not yet looked at) had legs of unequal length. I knew I had to share this, so I turned and spoke to the young lady behind me for less than a minute (the time it took for my panini to be heated). In that time, and I'm not sure how (except that God made a way out of my obedience) I managed to communicate to her that she might have problems with her back and her legs, which she confirmed (a little surprised, but pleasantly so).

Then I paid for my lunch, took it to a table and sat down. The table was not the most comfortable and there was a draft across the courtyard, so it was unlikely anyone would want to come and join me. But the lady I had spoken to in the queue came straight across with her lunch and asked if she could join me as she was amazed by what I had said to her earlier. She shared that at a recent wedding, her unequal leg length was so profound that the hem of her bridesmaid's dress had to be significantly altered to compensate for her condition. This led on to a conversation about Jesus who heals and I invited her across to the SOL stall at the Fayre. She received prayer and, in the space of a couple of minutes, Jesus completely restored her leg length and the pain left her back."

7. "Promised Land" prophecy. This exercise is partly symbolic and prophetically represents people crossing from their current situation, across the Jordan river, into the Promised Land to discover and take ownership of their blessings (Joshua 3 and 4). Divide people into two groups of equal number and place them in a line on opposite sides of the room, either side of an imaginary river. Provide supplies of blank paper and pens on each "bank" of the river and allow five minutes for each person to listen to God and write a strengthening, encouraging, comforting blessing on at least three different pieces of paper (without signing their name).

The "blessings" are placed face down on their side of the river.

When everyone is ready and all at the same time, everyone crosses the river into their Promised Land to receive their blessings. They do this by choosing three pieces of paper at random. I encourage people to walk around calmly asking God which piece of paper to pick up. The only rule is that once you have picked up and read a piece of paper, it is yours to keep. i.e. don't allow people to go "shopping" for something which confirms their own agenda. The results of this exercise are always amazing and people are so blessed by it.

8. Prophetic tables. This is an exercise we use at SOL specifically to prepare for our own organised spiritual fayres or attending psychic fayres, but it can be used by others. We normally have 70-80 people prophesying in our training sessions so we set up 8-10 small tables with two people at each table. One will be experienced and the other less so. The group leader will choose the experienced people and they in turn will pick someone from the rest of the group who is less experienced and will therefore be mentored through this exercise. The two people work together as recipients come and sit in front of them to receive words.

At the sound of a bell/whistle etc., a recipient will sit in front of the two people, who have three minutes to speak our words of life over the person. After three minutes the signal indicates that all recipients should vacate their seats and move on. The pattern repeats until everyone has been a recipient.

In order to keep engaged those people who have received, we normally welcome them to go through a prayer or "fire" tunnel. This gives an opportunity at the end of the exercise for the prophetic mentors and mentees to minister to each other, so that they can receive as well.

Running a prophetic presbytery

A prophetic "presbytery" is a gathering in which those with a prophetic gifting can bring insights and encouragement from God to a group of others. The apostle Paul recalls a prophetic presbytery (the word "presbytery" simply means "group of ministers") when he wrote to Timothy,

"Do not neglect your gift, which was given you through prophecy when the body of elders laid their hands on you." (1 Timothy 4:14)

Paula Price notes in her Prophet's Handbook, "A prophetic presbytery is alluded to or implied in Scripture through several mentions of a company of prophets (e.g. Samuel in 1 Samuel 10; Elisha in 2 Kings 2 and 4; also in Jeremiah 28 where the king summoned an apparent presbytery of prophets ... similar examples are seen with Ahab and Micaiah in 1 Kings 22 ..."

There are plenty examples from churches all over the world highlighting the fruit of prophetic presbyteries in the local church. Over the years I have personally received much from those at Catch The Fire, Toronto and Bethel Church, Redding.

Running a prophetic presbytery makes the prophetic so much more accessible and an important part of the life of the whole church. As ever, the focus should be on strengthening, encouraging and comforting the body. Again, rather than focusing on negatives, the purpose is to speak life into the members of the church. The presbytery may well unearth issues that later lead to ministry/ deliverance, but to maintain order it is a good discipline to allow a maximum of ten minutes per person.

The prophetic can work hand in hand with the prayer team, so that people requiring more prolonged ministry can be "handed over" and looked after. (If necessary, people may be referred to a more specialised ministry for inner healing, similar to Bethel Church's SOZO ministry). The presbytery is not there to spend extensive ministry time with one person.

In a small church, an easy model to follow is to invite people to sign up for ministry via the presbytery by giving their name to a designated administrator at the beginning of a meeting and being assigned a number. Thereafter, a bit like a post office, people wait to be served and go forward when their number is called.

It is helpful to state up front that people should not come back repeatedly for prophetic ministry, but wait at least two months before returning to the presbytery unless there are exceptional circumstances. On a practical level, this allows different people access to prophetic input and also provides space for guests from outside the church to attend and be ministered to. In addition, it allows adequate space and time for individuals to reflect on the words they've received, submit them to the accountability of trusted friends/leaders, and to rely on their own daily walk with the Lord, rather than relying on prophetic ministry as a substitute.

Helping the prophetic "genie"

The individual who insists on coming back time and again needs to be handled carefully and sensitively, so that they receive the help they need without monopolising the ministry team's time.

In the story of Aladdin, he would rub the magic lamp whenever he got into trouble, so that the genie would sort everything out. In the same way, people can tend to latch onto and seek out the "prophetic genie" whenever they want answers, guidance or when life is difficult or confusing. This may or may not be a wilful act, but it is not a healthy approach for either party. Our first response must always be to seek God, so that we mature in our relationship with him.

If, therefore, you feel a person's visits are becoming unusually frequent and they are persistent about being given a word, a kind, mature response is to direct them to the living word, highlighting that the Bible is full of words from God. Encourage them to read and apply the biblical truth. This is not abandoning pastoral responsibility, as deep pastoral issues can be handled in another context, but it protects the prophetic presbytery and keeps it doing what it is designed to do. In addition, it safeguards the prophets' time for their own family lives and walks with God.

The healthy prophetic team

Members of the prophetic team also need to safeguard their own individual walk with God. Part of a healthy team approach is to gather together before each presbytery meeting to receive any necessary cleansing and to be filled up before giving out. Team members can also encourage one another and help with each other's "up, in and out" relationships. i.e. up – we delight in God; in – our inner transformation; out – how we make a difference in the lives of others.

Welcoming the prophetic

In order for the prophetic to flourish in the church it must, of course, be welcomed by the leadership. Not only that, but it must be sufficiently high on the leadership's agenda so that it is given the time and space to operate.

Bill Johnson's teaching on testing the prophetic and holding onto that which is good is very useful in the process of welcoming the prophetic. One thing that can restrict the prophetic gift in the Church is the fear of false prophecy – and leaders having to deal with the ensuing fallout it may produce. Interestingly, there are more than 500 references to the word "prophet" in Scripture, but just 21 of these refer to a "false prophet". In other words, just under 5%. Paula Price makes the point that false prophecy was, and is, much less of an issue than people assume. "More damage is done," she says, "by the uneducated, such as those given little opportunity to perfect their skill." This is why in SOL we believe that great training is so important – and all the more so when it is given the space to be conducted under the godly authority of local church leadership.

The prophetic flourishes under godly leadership

The prophetic (as with all the five-fold ministries) flourishes under godly authority. Graham Cooke (in Developing Your Prophetic Gifting) comments that the prophetic ministry in the church is principally to confirm what we receive personally from the Lord in our own relationship with him and in his written word. Prophecy is not meant to replace this. He continues to say that this approach safeguards the relationship between church leadership and the prophetic ministry team. This is really important and a good safety net for "loose cannon" prophets who try to work outside the authority of the local church. Jim Goll writes, "God's intention ... is for the prophetic to operate in a team context of peers and friends, with mutual support being a blessing to one another. The safety net of a caring community and team ministry is a vital and necessary ingredient."

Prophet's reward

The Bible promises a great benefit to those who welcome the prophetic – an aspect that is probably not considered very much in contemporary churches. In Matthew 10:41 Jesus says,

"Whoever welcomes a prophet as a prophet will receive a prophet's reward, and whoever welcomes a righteous person as a righteous person will receive a righteous person's reward."

What is the prophet's reward? The ability to see in the Spirit and hear God. The process of placing value on the prophetic anointing and making space for it releases a grace that opens eyes and ears, resulting in an overall increase of the prophetic gift. Kris Vallotton says, "One often finds that the grace which accompany the prophets facilitates in the room an increased ability to hear the voice of the Holy Spirit."

Often we see an increase in the prophetic anointing in a congregation when a prophet is invited as a visiting speaker. How much more so when a church lives a lifestyle of welcoming the prophetic.

Prophetic roles in the local church

It is important that everyone understands the role the prophetic plays in the life of the church and the different levels of gifting that may function therein. Graham Cooke helpfully likens the role of prophecy in the church like a swimming pool.

"In the shallow end that all can safely use, is the inspirational prophetic gifting where our aim is to strengthen, encourage and comfort. It is usually nondirective, not correctional and seeks to bless (Paul's 'all can prophesy') and may be for sporadic one-off moments for a particular time and purpose. After the shallow end is the middle section where the water gets progressively deeper."

Some people will continue to function at the inspirational level, while others will gradually press into a deeper expression of the heart of God. They will move on from a casual use of the gift to nurture and hone it. The skill of bricklaying is a good analogy. Just because I lay a few bricks now and again in a reasonably straight line does not make me a bricklayer. But if I continue to learn the required techniques and apply the skills over time to increase speed, accuracy etc., then I may justifiably gain the title of "bricklayer".

With prophecy this means going deeper with God and trusting

him to receive more specific, revelatory type words, as opposed to general, inspirational ones. The application of this activity will include a wider range of people, scenarios and events, and will importantly begin to function outside of the local church (engaged in activities such as those we train for and apply in SOL).

Finally, Cooke addresses the role of the office of a prophet, in the very deep end of the swimming pool. This is the person who has continued, "going ever deeper into the supernatural realm of hearing God and being his mouthpiece. The prophet is concerned with holiness and purity and is seeking to prepare the bride of Christ ... speaking to churches, cities, regions and nations to ... church leaders, rulers and governments. His words will be accompanied by signs and wonders in healing miracles and clear signs of the supernatural presence of the Lord and His hosts." Kris Vallotton adds that the "Prophets have the authority to correct and direct because they are part of the government of God."

In a similar analogy, Jonathan Welton replaces the swimming pool of increasing depth with a simple triangle. The highest level (at the apex of the triangle) is the office of the prophet (Ephesians 4:11-13); the middle level is gift of prophecy (1 Corinthians 12:10) and the bottom level is faith i.e. where Paul says, "you can all prophesy" (1 Corinthians 14:31). In other words, everyone can prophesy, some have a gift of prophecy, and a few people have the calling of a prophet.

In the well known passage of Ephesians 4, we read that the fivefold ministries (apostles, prophets, evangelists, pastors and teachers) are given in order "...to equip his people for works of service, so that the body of Christ may be built up." Welton writes that the New Testament prophet is supposed to be equipping others for the work of the ministry. In other words, IF YOU ARE NOT EQUIPPING OTHERS IN PROPHECY THEN YOU ARE PROBABLY NOT A

PROPHET! Similarly, Kris Vallotton states that "the main function of a prophet is to equip the saints to do the work of service ... with eyes to see and ears to hear." Understanding our equipping role provides another safeguard which discourages loose cannon ministry, which is not primarily concerned with helping and enabling others.

A safe environment in which prophetic ministry can grow

SOL has served many churches by providing a safe place for people to activate and hone their prophetic gift. An increase in the number of sharp prophetic people can then have a positive influence on the growth of the prophetic in their own churches, gradually creating their own "safe places".

The safe environment consists of much mercy and patience for mistakes to be made, so that people can grow in confidence in their prophetic gifting without the fear of rebuke and rejection. Doesn't that mean there will be a bit of a mess at times? Of course, the answer is yes. As Proverbs 14:4 so directly puts it,

"Without oxen a stable stays clean, but you need a strong ox for a large harvest." (NLT)

In other words, the strength we need the oxen to provide comes at a price (listen to Bill Johnson's teaching "There are no poopless cows") – but we accept that the increase in strength is worth the occasional mess. As Mike Bickle comments, "Some prefer to have a ministry that is clean like the clean stables, even if it means losing the strength and increase that the prophetic ministry brings."

This does not mean that the prophetic gift should be allowed to operate without guidelines, which we have covered in earlier chapters. We follow the guidance of 1 Corinthians 14:40, "Everything should be done in a fitting and orderly way" and 1 Corinthians 14:32, "The spirits of the prophets are subject to the control of the prophets".

Kris Vallotton neatly sums up what we are aiming for with prophetic ministry in the church: mess with guidelines is symbolic of new life, whereas order without life is fruitless. "The most orderly place on the planet is the graveyard," he writes, "but there is no life there."

9

Putting It Into Practice

God is speaking to you now!

Yes, God is speaking to you and me now, right now. So now is a great time to step into becoming a speaker of life. Here are some steps to respond to this reality and help apply what you have been reading in this book. Remember, God is rejoicing and singing over you always, as in Zephaniah 3:17 reminds us (this scripture is engraved on the inside of my wedding ring):

"The Lord God is with you, He is mighty to save.
He will take great delight in you, He will quiet you with His love.
He will rejoice over you with singing".

Here we go!

1) Get some soaking music (see the recommended resources).

2) Get on your own

3) Have the Bible on hand as a reference. Remember that the "now", revelatory, Rhema word is based on the written, Logos word.

4) Get a notebook and pen or smartphone recorder.

5) As emphasised particularly by Mark Virkler, ask God the following three questions:
   a) what he thinks of you,
   b) ask him what he wants to say to you
   c) ask him what he would like you to do (if anything)
As your ears and heart are open, ask Father God if he has anything else for you, or someone else, or simply enjoy the love of Heaven pouring over you and seeping into your heart.

6) Quickly make a note of anything that distracts you – particularly things you suddenly remember you need to do. Now write down the answers to your three questions. Don't dwell on the answers so that your thought processes begin to get in the way, rather let the answers flow and write down your first impressions. It may be one word, a picture, a phrase, an impression. Draw it or speak it into your phone. The revelation may seem very subtle, like a butterfly landing, but record it anyway. If you find you have written a lot, use something like the dream interpretation template in Ch6 and highlight three important points.

7) Remember that if you submit to God and resist the devil, he must flee from you (James 4:7). You can trust the Holy Spirit to lead you into truth.

8) Remember the key points about the purpose and process of the prophetic word: purpose = SEC (strength, encouragement and comfort); process = RIA (revelation, interpretation and application).

Here is an example of the amazing things that can happen if you are obedient in seeking and listening to God. One SOL member caught a brief glimpse of Heaven. I hope it inspires you.

"During the first worship song I had a very clear vision of God taking me to a thick curtain and asking me if I wanted to go through it. I said YES! Immediately I found myself in an amazing place, which I knew was the Holy of Holies. It was an open vision, so I could see it whether my eyes were open or closed. In addition it affected all of my senses – I could actually hear a voice like the sound of rushing water (mentioned in both Ezekiel and Revelation). The rushing water voice was pure power and pure love!

I was aware of the complete universe and yet also the smallest, microscopic particle. I saw angels, amazing winds (angels are described like winds in Hebrews), moving rainbow colours and streams of living water in this place. Every drop of water seemed totally alive and full of light. It was AMAZING, I just kept looking.

Then I was shown some stepping stones stretching across the living water. I just had a strong desire to step out towards the intense love of my heavenly Daddy. I then realised that one simple step in the Holy of Holies represented an enormous stride in the earthly realm (i.e. a significant breakthrough). The steps across the river represented our calling/destiny which is set in our hearts (Ecclesiastes says that eternity is set in our hearts). Each step across the river seemed so easy as there was NO opposition to the step, no criticism, no resistance, no pride. There was simply a roar of encouragement, like the cloud of witnesses mentioned in Hebrews.

In this place, the Holy of Holies there was no criticism. All of this was outside, but inside there was pure joy and complete acceptance – a feeling of being totally where you were made to be."

Applying it beyond yourself

Having practiced receiving words of life ourselves, we naturally move on to speaking life over others.

Practice seeing with the eyes of Jesus. What do I mean by this? Ask God to give you insight into the "gold" that exists in others, that cannot be perceived superficially. Jesus saw the gold in his friend: Peter, the rock – and not the dirt: Simon, the broken reed.

Think of a person in your life with whom you have the most problems – conflict, irritancy, intimidation etc. Having developed a pattern of listening to and receiving from God, ask the Holy Spirit to reveal one aspect of gold in that person.

Now seek an opportunity to tell that person what you heard and observe how this positively affects/transforms your relationship. Cause and effect will mean that this practice becomes a greater part of your lifestyle.

Practice asking for a prophetic word for the person who is serving you in a café and then, if appropriate, bring this in to the normal flow of conversation in a relaxed way, to see if you heard correctly.

While this is happening, ask God if you are to do anything about this or is this just simply a training exercise. You can also practice this kind of scenario with a friend you meet for coffee. Practice on each other and then you give honest feedback and encouragement.

Establishing a daily rhythm

As you become accustomed to the pattern of the above, why not begin to "prophesy your day" by asking the Lord each morning when you wake up for information about something that will happen during your day. Assess this at the end of the day and make a note of how well you participated and understood. Remember there is no condemnation in Christ Jesus (Romans 8:1), so don't beat yourself up if you have missed some opportunities – it's all part of the training process. Value the process, not just the end result.

Today, take time to practice God's presence. Intentionally prioritise him. Rush to and welcome his incredible presence in each sphere of influence where you find yourself in your daily living. Pray and expect God himself to invade the place, Heaven on earth right here, right now!

I feel moved by the Holy Spirit to encourage you to pray in tongues right now for 5, 10, 20, 30, 60 minutes (however long you have). That heavenly language will have amazing spiritual breakthrough implications for your day and destiny. The Holy Spirit wants to move powerfully through your life, to enable you to convey the life-changing Gospel through love, signs, wonders and miracles.

Leading people to the Lord

As you foster the prophetic lifestyle there will many scenarios where people will be experiencing God on the outside and want to have God on the inside, 24/7. We should practice and be prepared with a simple salvation prayer to help. Here is an ABCD salvation prayer as an example:

A) Admit you have been living your life your way and not God's way (the Bible calls this being a sinner). "All have sinned and come short of the glory of God" (Romans 3:23).

B) Believe that Jesus is the son of God and he died on the cross for your sins and rose from the dead. "Believe on the Lord Jesus Christ, and you will be saved" (Acts 16:31). "But God demonstrates his own love for us in this: while we were still sinners, Christ died for us" (Romans 5:8). And, of course, John 3:16.

C) Confess and repent of your sins (be sorry and turn away from them) and receive God's forgiveness. "If we confess our sins, he is faithful and just to forgive our sins" (1 John 1:9). Also Ephesians 2:8-9.

D) Decide to accept Jesus as your loving Lord and Saviour. "If you declare with your mouth, 'Jesus is Lord,' and believe in your heart that God raised him from the dead, you will be saved. For it is with your heart that you believe and are justified, and it is with your mouth that you profess your faith and are saved" (Romans 10:9-10).

In Ezekiel 37:4-5 God spoke prophetically, instructing Ezekiel to, "Prophesy to these bones and say to them, 'Dry bones, hear the word of the Lord... I will make breath enter you, and you will come to life!'". Prophetically he speaks the same over you! Romans 4:17 calls the Lord, "the God who gives life to the dead and calls things that are not as though they were." Allow his promises and prophetic words over you to ignite and fuel you and your circumstances, becoming the dynamite (dunamis) for your prayers.

Practice speaking life over your diary, over your destiny, over your relationships, over your body, over your circumstances. Every day, BE A SPEAKER OF LIFE!

10 Recommended Resources

Bibliography/Recommended books

Understand Your Dreams Now: spiritual dream interpretation, Doug Addison, eGenCo publishers, 2013.

The Seer: The prophetic power of Visions, Dreams and Open Heavens, Jim Goll, Destiny Image Publishers, 2005.

The School of Seers: a practical guide on how to see in the unseen realm, Jonathan Welton, Destiny Image Publishers, 2013.

Spiritual Discernment and the Mind of Christ, Francis Frangipane, Arrow Publications Inc., 2013.

Activating Your Prophetic Gift, Kevin Horn, Open Heavens Revival Press, 2013.

There Is Always Enough, Heidi Baker, Sovereign World, 2003.

Learning To Love, Rolland & Heidi Baker, River Publishing & Media, 2012.

Birthing the Miraculous: The Power of Personal Encounters with God to Change Your Life and the World, Heidi Baker, Charisma House, 2014.

The Prophet's Handbook: A guide to prophecy and its operation, Paula A. Price, Whitaker House, 2008.

The Prophet's Dictionary: The ultimate guide to supernatural wisdom, Paula A. Price, Whitaker House, 2006.

Growing in the Prophetic, Mike Bickle, Charisma House, 2008.

Developing Your Prophetic Gifting, Graham Cooke, Sovereign World, 1994.

Union and Communion: a commentary on the Song of Songs, J. Hudson Taylor (republished by Alpha international, Holy Trinity Brompton, London)

You May All Prophesy, Steve Thompson, MorningStar Publications, 2007.

Prophetic Ministry, Rick Joyner, MorningStar Publications, 2007.

The Prophet's Notebook, Barry Kissell, Kingsway Publications, 2002.

Moving in the Prophetic, Greg Haslam, Monarch Books, 2009.

Basic Training for the Prophetic Ministry, Kris Vallotton, Destiny Image Publishers, 2011.

Angelic Encounters: engaging help from Heaven, James and Michal Ann Goll, Charisma House, 2007.

Dream Language: The prophetic power of dreams, revelations and the spirit of wisdom, James and Michal Ann Goll, Destiny Image Publishers, 2006.

The Ultimate Treasure Hunt, Kevin Dedmon, Destiny Image Publishers, 2007.

When Heaven Invades Earth, Bill Johnson, Destiny Image Publishers, 2007.

The Grace Outpouring, Roy Godwin, Kingsway Communications, 2011.

Invading Babylon: the seven mountain mandate, Lance Wallnau and Bill Johnson, Destiny Image Publishers, 2013.

Fire of the North: the life of St Cuthbert, David Adam, SPCK Publishing, 2003.

Britain's Spiritual Inheritance, Diana Chapman, River Publishing and Media, 2012.

Recommended teaching courses, online sources and soaking music

Rick Joyner and morning Star ministries:
www.morningstarministries.org

John Paul Jackson and Stream Ministries:
http://www.streamsministries.com

o Basics of Dreams, Visions and Strange Events – John Paul Jackson
o The Biblical Model of Dream Interpretation – John Paul Jackson
o Prophets and Psychics – John Paul Jackson
o Understanding Dreams and Visions – John Paul Jackson

Doug Addison Ministries
http://dougaddison.com
o The Dream Crash Course

James Goll and Network Ministries
http://encountersnetwork.com/index.html

Bethel Church Ministries, Redding, USA
http://bethelredding.com

John and Carol Arnott
http://www.johnandcarol.org/

Catch the Fire Ministries
http://www.catchthefire.com

Dr Mark Virkler [on listening to God's voice]
www.cwgministries.org

The Elijah List
https://www.elijahlist.com

There are no poopless cows, audio message, Bill Johnson, Bethel store.

Glasgow Prophetic Centre
www.glasgow-prophetic-centre.org.uk/

Light and Life
http://www.lightlife.org.uk/index.html

Fflad y brenin
http://www.ffald-y-brenin.org/

Northumbrian Centre of Prayer for Christian Healing
http://www.christian-healing.com/

Wholeness Through Christ
http://www.wholenessthroughchrist.org/

Julie True online soaking
http://julietrue.com/online-healing-room

The Riveras soaking music
http://kimberlyandalbertorivera.com/home.cfm

How to connect with SOL:
e-mail: speakersoflife.tic@hotmail.co.uk
Facebook: www.facebook.com/speakersoflife
Website: www.speakersoflife.org

Made in the USA
Monee, IL
17 August 2020

38664564R00098